MISS LIT

FOR LIFE LESSONS

LESSONS FOR HIGH SCHOOL
ENGLISH TEACHERS
BY A HIGH SCHOOL
ENGLISH TEACHER

MICOLE WILLIAMS

Publisher, Eclectically You Experience, LLC in the United States of America
www.eclecticallyyou.com

© 2019 by Micole Williams
English Teacher
Micole@eclecticallyyou.com
Twitter @MissLit4Life
Blog misslit4lifeenglishteacher.wordpress.com

Cataloging-in Publication Data is on file at Library of Congress

Paperback ISBN 978-1-7333023-2-6

First printing, 2020

Cover and Interior Design Micole Williams
Production Micole Williams
Editor Kionna LeMalle
Associate Editor Geri Felder

CROSSING GENRES

HIGHWAY ANALYSIS

STORY CENTRAL

PERSUASIVE PARKWAY

REFLECTION AVENUE

CONTENTS

FOREWORD

All English teachers need a book like this. Students change. Demographics shift. Freedoms and limitations hang on a swinging pendulum. But always, lessons that challenge students appropriately, integrate reading and writing effectively, and leave room for personal connection, lead to high levels of growth.

In search of such lessons, teachers seek guidance from colleagues who have successfully overcome similar challenges and have met the needs of diverse populations of students. In Micole Williams, we find such a colleague, and here she has curated activities proven effective across grade levels in five different high schools—each unique in student make-up, faculty culture, and available resources.

In *Miss Lit for Life Lessons*, Micole's voice leaps off of the page. It is as though we are sitting at the planning table with a mentor, letting us know we are safe, affirming our calling even when we feel stressed, and challenging us to try something new. What most sets this book apart, however, is Micole's inclusion of self-care tips combined with the Scripture references that have carried her through the hard work of teaching. There is a thread of total reliance on God throughout the book. This thread is not didactic, preachy, or evangelical, but it carries with it a sense of transparency that makes *Miss Lit for Life Lessons* a trusted friend.

In my twenty-three years as an educator, I have worked in many different capacities—classroom teacher, college professor, instructional coach, and curriculum coordinator. What I have found to be most consistent is a need to balance the deeply personal and deftly professional work of teaching, with a spiritual dependence on God that kicks in at the point of burn out and keeps teachers going when the work gets hard. And the work always gets hard.

In *Miss Lit for Life Lessons*, you won't find scripts, scopes and sequences, or carefully structured scaffolds. You will find what all English teachers at some point need: lessons to supplement your existing curriculum, tips for managing the ELA classroom, suggestions for self-care, and opportunity for spiritual renewal.

Turn the page.
Plan for success.
Find fresh energy in the pages of this book.
Get *lit for life!*

Sincerely,

Kionna LeMalle, M.Ed.
Editor

DEAR TEACHER,

You may be a rookie who needs direction, a vet who needs rerouting, a sudden homeschool educator who needs a break, or a teacher relocating and in need of unfussy transferable lessons. Wherever you are at THIS moment...

A new journey awaits! A new adventure is ahead. Your path is yours. With your students,
you are a guide for their exploration. I am glad you have chosen this book to help you navigate.

Between you and me, I don't wish my first two or even three years of teaching on my worst enemy. Three different schools. The first: A spirited predominately-black school where I taught senior English and a first-time yearbook class (with no school cameras). The second: A preppy predominately-white school where I taught sophomores and travelled with a push cart to three different rooms daily. The third: A revamped, charter school in a small town where I was the one and ONLY high school ELA teacher. Three different schools. Three different types of rules. I felt like a fool rather than the master of my fate and rightfully so. I was up against many antagonistic forces, and all I was trying to do was teach English Language Arts.

I will admit, it took me years to find my groove in the classroom. I was a *goodie two shoes* student, but as a teacher, somehow, I was always in the principal's office. A rebel with a cause. An introverted misfit. A misunderstood empath. My brand of care looked different from my colleagues. I didn't fit naturally into the traditional teacher world. I found it to be a bit outdated, uninspiring, and contradicting. It may have been that I minored in English and majored in mass communications which ultimately meant I degreed in an open-ended question. I saw things differently. It may have been because I jumped around every two years within my first six years. Or it may have been more. It was just an interesting time.

Early on, my attempts to teach seemed futile. My support seemed far away. Though my mom and my grandmother successfully retired in the field, and even went back to teach after retirement, I didn't think I had the finesse. By my third year, I feared teaching was not *my* thing. I had done my best, and it was a nightmare. I was tired of crying. After my first two years of attempting to teach, I really wanted to quit. And I did.

But God...God has a weird sense of humor. During my sabbatical, I worked on some passion projects and became an author of a fiction novel and an indie filmmaker. While looking for work outside of education, a new teaching job found me. The far-away charter school paid far less than my starting salary at my previous district. I took the job due to no luck elsewhere. It was such a small campus, I was the only ELA teacher. Here was another challenge: teaching four different grade levels meant four different core preps. But that wasn't enough. I also taught Professional Communications and Test Prep. My administrators really put all of my certifications to use. God had a lesson plan I could not deny. I learned that no matter how much you move around, much will be the same. He showed me a way through what felt like an overwhelming maze, and I learned how to incorporate old and new practices while creating more personalized lessons for my students. Lo and behold, it was a breakthrough moment. I actually learned how to teach.

After that experience, I went on to teach at two schools, both large and diverse. The last was finally close to home. Now after 12 years, I guess you can say, life happened while I was teaching. I can look back at my years in the classroom and see what I accomplished. I weathered many storms while teaching various grade levels. I helped many students grow in engagement, productivity, and skill. I prepared my students for standardized tests and high-stakes writing. Across student demographics and individual needs, my students showcased improved scores as evidence of growth. I gladly tracked students' ideas about what contributed most to their learning, and I have added these student favorites to this book. Most recently, in a pandemic, impromptu virtual class was in session, and now, I'm on to the next chapter, teaching ELA in this fashion, for my current school.

Here, I share the lessons (professional and personal) that I know have been the most effective as I watched one year of teaching change into three years, four into seven, ten and now twelve. I offer *Miss Lit for Life Lessons* to you, dear teacher, as a year-round, modern-day survival kit for high school English/Language Arts. Whether you teach in the classroom, online, or at home, you will find a decade of what has worked for many different types of students and situations.

I am proof that a rocky road can lead to not only finding your way, but creating a roadmap for others to navigate and travel in their own unique classrooms.

Sincerely,

Micole Williams
Micole Williams,
Miss Lit 4 Life

HOW TO USE THE BOOK

The book is designed so you can utilize it *as is* or customize for your 21st-century learner. Within *Miss Lit for Life Lessons*, you will find a variety of timeless go-to assignments that can be applied to the ever changing landscape of teaching and across various grade levels. These pages include a balance of versatile, real-world reading, writing, and communication challenges that encourage students to *actually work*, as well as strategic activities that build stamina for standardized tests. Peppered in, you will also find additional year-long accessories to take advantage of while making copies or brewing coffee. The book is not intended to reflect a full scope, nor must the lessons unfold in a predetermined sequence. Rather, this book provides a supporting aid to English teachers that can easily supplement any existing curriculum to add variety, challenge, and to meet students' unique needs.

Begin by reading the "Dear Teacher" letter at the start of each chapter. In this letter you will find:
+ Self-care tips
+ Inspiration to keep going
+ Simple classroom management advice to save time

In each chapter, you will see a mix of planning and lesson tabs. Here's how to use the personally crafted, easy-to-use challenges for your high school ELA students:
+ Check out the specific activities found in the chapter above the planning tab.
+ Locate the first page of each new challenge, using the lesson tab.
+ Read a short reflection from my classroom perspective above each lesson tab.
+ Use my planning grid for an overview of the benefits, outcomes, and materials needed to implement each challenge.
+ Print or blow up the genre-specific graphic for your classroom or door decor.
+ Have fun, be flexible, and bring your energy and creativity to your classroom.

The heart and goal of this book is to empower teachers to guide students through a multitude of literary challenges that give them experience in taking ELA into the real world.

Let's Stay Connected...

How did you use these challenges in your class?
Share your thoughts, experiences, and results!

Thank you for joining this "Lit for Life" journey!

I post resources and references I use on my blog and Twitter page.

Micole Williams
Twitter @MissLit4Life
Blog misslit4lifeenglishteacher.wordpress.com
#misslit4lifelessons

Have an awesome school year!

CROSSING GENRES

DEAR TEACHER,

What really made things come full circle for me had a lot to do with *getting* and *keeping* my classroom in order. Here are some intentional traditions I learned to set within the first days of class because they served a clear purpose throughout the year.

- Incorporating **MEMES** to display info in class and on syllabus for not-so-fun literature (like class rules / expectations)
- Hanging **visible "late work" and "make up" work folders** on the side of my desk serves as a tracking system of habits, work, and accountability. Having students title their own work "late" when it is accepted after the deadline keeps communication clear by providing a record of when I received items.
- Having **students sign up for tutorials** in advance instead of just showing up makes the commitment feel more official. It also allows me to prepare adequate work, so the tutorials can run effectively if multiple students show up and need one-on-one attention.
- Using a **planning template** that can be customized easily helps to ensure all literacy processes are incorporated. Two years ago, our 10th grade team adopted **ELA gurus, Kelly Gallagher and Penny Kittle's** template from ***180 Days*** for daily student practices: read, write, study, create, and then share.
- Setting up a **Reward System** helps foster motivation when students get overwhelmed or distracted. I love the Olympics, so my students get medals for academic achievement (while I play theme music) plus work displayed on the medalists' board.

SCRIPTURE

"Having gifts that differ according to the grace given to us, let us use them: if prophecy, in proportion to our faith; If service, in our serving; the one who teaches, in his teaching."
Romans 12:6-7

INSPIRATION

"A good leader inspires people to have confidence in the leader. A great leader inspires people to have confidence in themselves."
Eleanor Roosevelt

Getting to know you activities can definitely be fun, but do not have to be absent of rigor...

I've learned the *mushier* the getting-to-know-you activities are, the *harder* the year will be. I've also learned that when I jump into content, full throttle, there is less push back. Students know what to expect from the first day. Setting the tone early creates an ethos that carries the class throughout the year.

By blending some high-tech 21st-century literacy skills with traditional reading and writing, this section will help you do that! Being a person who loves competition, I refer to my lessons as challenges from the very beginning. Start on the first day with meaningful and fun challenges that allow students to showcase their unique attributes and abilities.

We all know that the first days are first impressions for both teacher and student. We also know that the first week is crucial for establishing social norms and foundational aspects in this lush English Language Arts world. My mission has always been to utilize my growing love and experience for **literature, speech, and media** by mixing these elements, helping students connect and apply them not only in my class, but in the real-world!

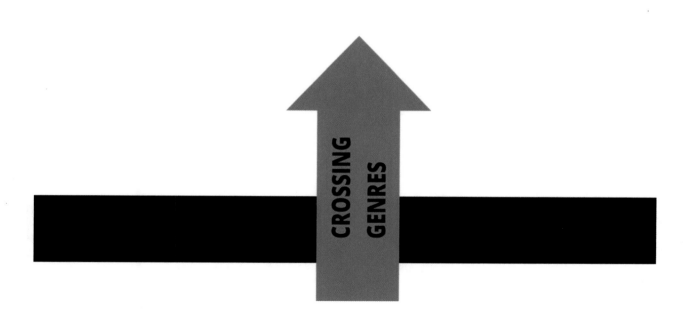

CROSSING GENRES

READY, SET, GO!

Grossing Genres Activities

+ Create your Class Twitter Page
(Symbolism)

+ Use Vision Boards in the Classroom
(Motifs and Allusions)

+ Rewrite History
(Style +)

+ Connect Genres
(Theme, Plot, Allusions, Motifs)

...my recent classroom and the vision board categories students could pick from...

The Digital Superstars:

MODERN-DAY
ELA

Create Your Class Twitter Page

Students often assume their teacher is the audience when they write. I always want students to wrap their minds around the idea of writing for a specific audience, the general public, and a global audience. One way I get this point across is by utilizing social media platforms. In this case, I use Twitter to challenge them to introduce themselves to the world in a succinct and symbolic manner.

Benefits	**Preparation**
This activity allows for the digital interactivity the students crave while serving as a great tool to measure their understanding of each unit's content. Students actively engage in processing new content while practicing written communication.	- A live online teacher sample (finished product) - A template with a grade-point sheet built-in (rough draft) - An alternative: Students who don't have permission to create a Twitter page can create a computer-generated version that mimics the site and answers the objectives.
After the session,	**Materials**
After class Twitter profiles are created, I create challenges once a month or at the start or end of a unit (ie. **post links of articles related to the reading, music videos or poetry that connect theme, own original work, comments to others, etc.)**	- A common online area where students can access a template and upload their own draft for review (I use Google Classroom) - Computer devices/ cell phones to access social media - School credentials (email login directions, classroom codes) Tip: *Keep these for new students*.

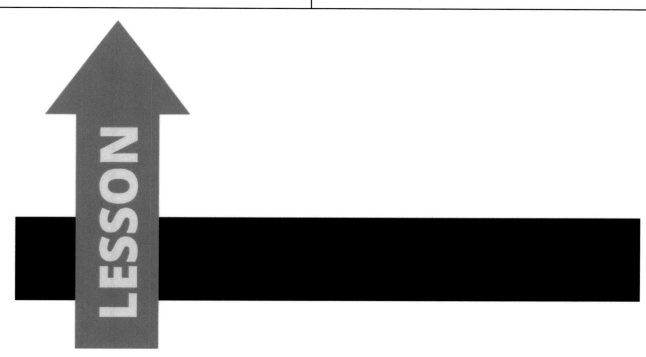

LESSON

Create Your Class Twitter Page

Before creating a live/real Twitter page,
create a draft here that I can double-check to make sure you don't have typos, errors, etc.
Those who don't have parent permission have adjusted directions.
Using your school account, you can proceed when your draft is approved.

For this Daily grade:
You can earn
20 points for a Symbolic Picture
This is not a photo of you but instead a symbol of who you are.

ie.

20 points for a Symbolic name that explains the picture
This is not your real name but a name that represents who you are.
At the end, add the period I have you in my class.
Create a name @_#per

ie.

MissLit4Life
@MissLit4Life

20 points for your symbolic tagline
Create a tagline that shares a bit about you and includes the following:
1. a colon :
2. a comma series that includes 3 characteristics

ie. a native Houstonian who enjoys what she calls being lit for life: a teacher by profession, a writer by heart, and an optimist by nature!

40 points Your first Twitter challenge will be to post your answer.
MissLit4Life@MissLit4Life

Your Turn!

Create Your Class Twitter Page

On Online Platform _____

COMPLETE Your Rough Draft Here and
CLICK "TURN IN" BY THE DEADLINE

Using your school account, before creating a live/real Twitter page,
create a draft here that I can double-check and approve.

20 points for a Symbolic Picture

INSERT or Copy and PASTE (Save this picture on your computer/phone to be able to use later)

20 points for Symbolic name that explains the picture

TYPE YOUR ANSWER, FOLLOWING INSTRUCTIONS ABOVE

20 points for your symbolic tagline

TYPE YOUR ANSWER, FOLLOWING INSTRUCTIONS ABOVE

40 points Get ready to post your answer. The challenge will be posted soon.

Follow/post with your school account only @_____**(teacher's account)**

Use Vision Boards in the Classroom

I am a big fan of vision boards which can be used as a tool for engagement, analysis, discussion and empowerment. **The Law of Attraction states that *regardless of age, nationality or religious belief, we each have the ability to attract into our lives whatever we are focusing on.*** It's been an honor and a lot of fun presenting how to use vision boards in the classroom to other teachers within our district.

Benefits With an honest approach to one's dreams/ wishes/goals, I found creating vision boards to be a great way to get to know my students while teaching the **skills** below: - Nuance - Symbolism and Motif - Reference and Allusion.	**Prepare** - Presentation of slides or handouts that cover process, skills assessed, and rubric - Teacher model of a vision board - Student samples from past years or from family to help show diverse options and styles
After the crafty session, I assigned presentation time for students to share elements of their vision board and find an accountability partner in the class who would check in with them or help them stay on top of one of their goals. It also served as a way for their classmates to bond and support each other.	**Materials** - Posters & printer paper - Scissors - Markers & colored pencils - Pens & pencils - Tape/ Glue sticks/ Liquid Glue - Variety of magazines **You will find** - Exact slides from my presentation - Graphic organizers for brainstorming

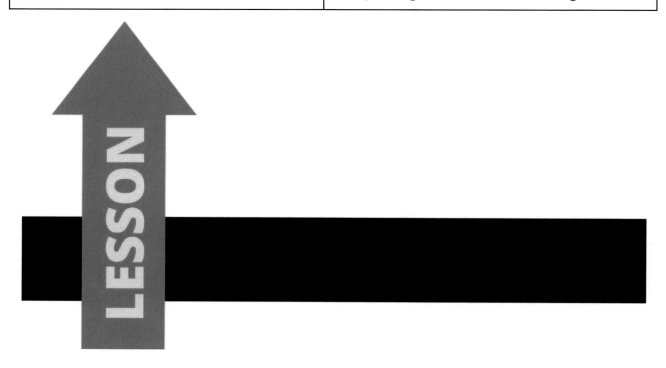

How do I want my year to look and feel in various areas of MY life?

It's MANIFESTATION TIME:

Creation of
vision board with rubric

NUANCES:
What is the difference between...
A SYMBOL AND A MOTIF?

A REFERENCE AND AN ALLUSION?

motif: a recurrent feature/symbol/ dominant idea captured in an artistic or literary composition

allusion: a figure of speech that refers to a well-known story, event, person, or object, in order to make a connection in one's mind.

1. **Find examples of both in various texts.**
2. **Be prepared to share your findings.**

Vision Board Creation Prep:

Connect Visuals and Quotes
for Each Category

What is the origin or significance of these illustrations?
What are the advantages of using symbols?
What can visuals do that words can't?

WHAT IS THE ORIGIN OR SIGNIFICANCE OF THESE ILLUSTRATIONS?

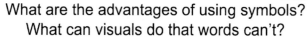

What are the advantages of using symbols?
What can visuals do that words can't?

WHAT'S THE ORIGIN OF THIS QUOTE OR ALLUSION?

WORD BANK

Star Wars Movie?
Les Brown?
Gone with the Wind Movie?
Eleanor Roosevelt?
Jerry Maguire Movie?
Dr. Martin Luther King, Jr?
Casablanca Movie?

WHAT ARE THE ADVANTAGES OF USING ALLUSIONS INSTEAD OF LITERAL WORDING?

Think about the answers and what do these people/ movies represent?

I too "Have A Dream"

"After all, tomorrow is another day"

"Show me the money!"

"We'll always have Paris"

"To handle yourself, use your head; to handle others, use your heart."

"Too many of us are not living our dreams because we are living our fears."

May the force be with you."

What are the advantages of using allusions instead of literal wording?

I too "Have A Dream"
Dr. Martin Luther King, Jr
"After all, tomorrow is another day"
Gone with the Wind Movie
"Show me the money!"
Jerry Maguire Movie
"We'll always have Paris"
Casablanca Movie
"To handle yourself, use your head; to handle others, use your heart."
Eleanor Roosevelt
"Too many of us are not living our dreams because we are living our fears."
Les Brown
May the force be with you."
Star Wars Movie

Vision Board Creation Prep: Reflect on Last Year

My top achievement of the year	What did I learn?	What were distractions/ mission blocks?	Who were people I learned from/people who inspired?
How did I make myself feel great?	What was my most common negative emotion?	How do I feel about my progress?	What did I not make happen?
What fears did I encounter?	What were some of the greatest insights I gathered this year?	On a scale from 1-5, how present was I? How often was I invested in the moment?	Note to self:

Assessment
Score yourself on a scale from 1-5....(1 = poor 3 = fair and 5 = awesome)

Attitude ____Spiritual ____Mind ____Personal growth____
Career and Business ____$$$ ____Fitness ____Health ____
Relationships ____Family ____Fun and Social____

Create Your Vision Board

Give yourself permission to get clear about your vision and nurture your vision!
Create a board that is a visual representation of what you want to manifest
(or how you want your year to go).

Check out the 11 categories - Choose 10 to use (refer to teacher model and rubric).
Attitude ____Spiritual ____Mind ____Personal growth____
Career and Business ____$$$ ____Fitness ____Health ____
Relationships ____Family ____Fun and Social____

Effectively use inspiration from others: the web, stories, songs, etc.
Properly cite your references.

Let the categories serve as areas in your life you'd like to focus on.
In a balanced and presentable way, showcase a combination of specific words and
meaningful pictures that each represent what you envision for this year in those areas.

Vision Board Aftermath

During this writing time,
refer back to your completed vision board.
Reflect and thoroughly answer the questions below.
Share your insight later in a Socratic Seminar discussion.

1.   How does the author's words inspire you? Why?

2.   How does the artist's visual empower you? Why?

3.   What area/category is your strongest? Weakest? Why?

4.   How could you use an accountability partner this year?

Rewrite History:
Put a modern-day spin on an old piece

What is style again? Voice? I am sure we have all heard this too often. How can we make conversations about voice and style more meaningful? Make answers more concrete? I want my students to understand that the distinctive sound of the author is the author's voice, and we come to know this unique voice as the author's style. I have found it is best to spend less time trying to explain this and more time throwing my students into work that fosters this deeper understanding. By giving the task of recreating or reimagining a pre-existing piece with a distinct voice, I offer my students the opportunity to pay attention to details that help them determine the author's style. In *Voice Lessons: Classroom Activities to Teach Diction, Detail, Imagery, Syntax, and Tone*, Nancy Dean explains, "[Voice] is the expression of who we are ... the fingerprint of a person's language. Through voice we come to know authors; by exploring voice, we learn to wield language. The aim ... is for each student to better develop a personal voice: to do so, a student must first learn to recognize voice and analyze its elements" (xi).

Here, you'll find:
- A **rewriting activity with a menu of options** for students to pick from that will give them practice working with details and elements that shape voice and determine style.

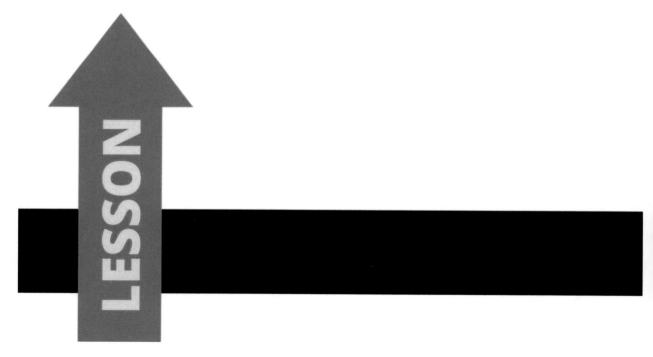

Rewrite History

Put a modern-day spin on an old piece

Choose your make-over challenge...

THE BEFORE	THE AFTER
1. Find an old magazine article	and put a new spin on it in the form of a blogpost
2. Take an old song with outdated slang or faddish items;	revamp it with words and objects that speak for your generation
3. Take an old newspaper article	and rewrite the predicament as a fictional piece instead
4. Take a classic advertisement	and satirize it
5. Find a scene from a script	give it a remix

Connect Genres

We all have our favorite books, shows, films, and songs. These favorites are useful when teaching **theme** by challenging students to identify and expand on central messages across genres and mediums. They are also useful for revisiting earlier skills: **motifs** and **allusions**.

In my class, I like to challenge students to connect four stories through themes. I provide the actual theme for my models in class (i.e. *sometimes love loses the fight against outside forces, true friendship survives the harshest realities, etc.*). The students are responsible for determining other details. I let my students do research in order to find a variety of possible answers to complete the charts.

I am providing a template that can be uploaded to your online classroom, projected, or given as a hard copy. Students should use this model to generate their own online or hard copy version.

Here, you'll find:
- A **Genre Connections template** for students to use

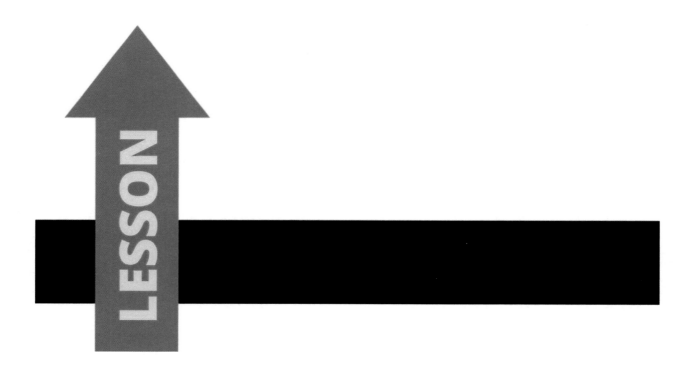

Create a computer-generated version of your own samples.

Title of the piece:_____
"Allusion"_____

Motif

PICTURE

Write a sentence that notes:
the Genre, Medium, Title, Era
and Plot Premise of the piece

Title of the piece:_____
"Allusion"_____

Motif

PICTURE

Write a sentence that notes:
the Genre, Medium, Title, Era
and Plot Premise of the piece

1   2
GENRE CONNECTIONS
3   4

Title of the piece:_____
"Allusion"_____

Motif

PICTURE

Write a sentence that notes:
the Genre, Medium, Title, Era
and Plot Premise of the piece

Title of the piece:_____
"Allusion"_____

Motif

PICTURE

Write a sentence that notes:
the Genre, Medium, Title, Era
and Plot Premise of the piece

HIGHWAY ANALYSIS

DEAR TEACHER,

I believe in exposing students to various resources so they can get the facts they need to form their own substantiated opinions. I provide go-to resources for student binders at the beginning of the year. I hold my students responsible for keeping up with these year-long reference sheets. I have peppered these throughout this book, but most are in this section. Providing all **year-round resources/strategies** at the beginning of the year gives students a sense of our shared purpose and initiates an early need to get and maintain supplies. I stress that I will not give out second copies to high schoolers (though I do put some online so they can replenish.)

Sometimes, a class set will do. I create a class set of TONE packets students can use on an as-needed basis to enhance their writing. I make copies of tone word banks with a hundred plus words to choose from, including words that are positive, negative, and neutral. I staple them in a folder labeled "Tone Packet."

We know what a difference seating arrangements make. I set my classroom up strategically. In early stages of discussion, I arrange students in small groups. But when it is time for whole class discussion, arranging the class in a circle is a powerful way to:
1. Equalize students,
2. Promote focused dialogue,
3. Visually demonstrate that this is not only a student-centered class, but each student can have the floor.

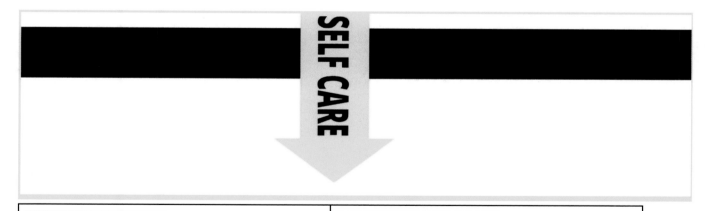

SCRIPTURE

"While we look not at the things which are seen, but at the things which are not seen: for the things which are seen *are* temporal; but the things which are not seen *are* eternal."
2 Corinthians 4:18

INSPIRATION

"If you dig deeply, you will find that you are not a singular self but that there are many selves, many voices within you. The more conscious you are of those selves and the more you let them find expression through you, the more complete you will be."
Frederick Lenz

What can analysis often feel like in the classroom?
Students: Like digging for buried treasure
Teachers: Like pulling teeth...

Our peers often express their anxiety and students sometimes groan with reluctance when asked to read between the lines.

Why?

Unlike other core subjects in which closed-ended questions rule, in ELA there are a multitude of potentially correct answers. Accuracy is in thoughtful evidence and meaningful reflection.

Whether on paper or through dialogue, when digging deeper, one must have the right tools. Once the atmosphere is set for embracing open-ended questions and various substantiated viewpoints, our students are rewarded by uncovering their very own treasures.

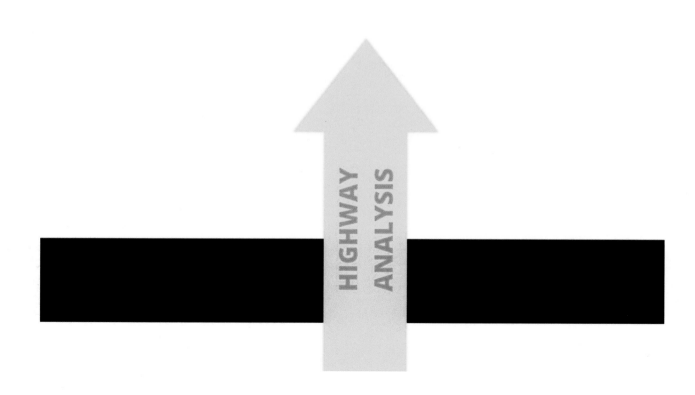

HIGHWAY ANALYSIS

READY, SET, GO!

Highway Analysis Activities

Bonus: What does an author do?
Active Verbs Resource

+ Employ Williams' Note-taking in 3D
(WN3D for Rhetorical Analysis)

+ Make Colorful Sandwiches
(Color-Coded Analytical Paragraphs)

+ Cross-over Analytical Paragraphs
(Make Connections)

+ Facilitate Book-of-Choice Discussions
(Literary Questions)

+ Host a Lit-for-Life Lounge
(Poetry and Prose)

+ Appreciate Art in ELA
("In-Class" Field Trips to the Museum)

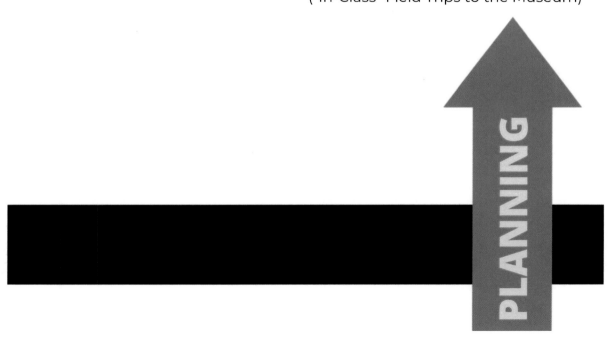

PLANNING

...my past classroom, my 3rd year as a teacher, when I taught 4 grade levels at a charter school...

The WHY is made up of each grade level's set of burning questions which they assigned themselves to answer through research and analysis...

HIGHWAY ANALYSIS

ENGLISH LANGUAGE ARTS

RESOURCE: What does the author do?

When analyzing an author's work, use vivid verbs. Most of the words in this word bank can replace "says" and "does" - which are overused and flat. They also can be used to share what a character or subject is doing.

Example: With a comforting tone, Collins <u>explores</u> how ideas of the past can <u>inform</u> our future.

Example: King effectively <u>guides</u> the reader through a maze of details in order to later <u>reveal</u> the truth is hiding in plain sight.

				ADD YOUR OWN
adapts	constructs	expresses	obtains	
addresses	contributes	extends	pacifies	
admits	conveys	gains	produces	
applies	coordinates	galvanizes	progresses	
aids	correlates	generalizes	promotes	
aligns	creates	generates	prompts	
alleviates	critiques	guides	qualifies	
alters	crystallizes	illuminates	questions	
amplifies	elaborates	illustrates	reasons	
asserts	eliminates	imagines	reassures	
assesses	emphasizes	immobilizes	reciprocates	
associates	employs	implements	recognizes	
assumes	encompasses	incorporates	recommends	
attains	engages	increases	refines	
attracts	enhances	Indicates	represents	
attributes	enlarges	influences	resolves	
augments	ensures	initiates	simplifies	
avoids	entails	integrates	suggests	
captures	equips	magnifies	supports	
challenges	establishes	maintains	surpasses	
characterizes	evaluates	manages	surprises	
claims	evolves	marvels	sustains	
clarifies	examines	merits	uncovers	
compiles	exemplifies	notices	upholds	
compresses	exhibits	nourishes	values	
conceives	expands	nurtures	views	
conducts	experiences	obliges		
connects	explores	observes		

Employ Williams' Note- Taking in 3D:
Use WN3D for Rhetorical Analysis

I made a breakthrough my first year teaching seniors. I can remember like it was yesterday, but it was 2007. The occasion: My first evaluation. I wasn't sure what I should prepare. I wanted to teach something that was actually going to be used after the evaluation. As a team, we were teaching seniors from the textbook. I knew students had taken a lot of notes, but I also knew how ineffective notes were if they were not actually being used. I hated linear notes with a passion. So I created a note-taking system that made it easier to take notes while thinking deeply about content.

My appraiser and my certification program mentor came in on the same day. I felt intense pressure. I remember using Shakespearen sonnets as the text. The topic was *Time can't change love*. I walked seniors through, for the first time, a system I would use, in some form or fashion, for the rest of my career. Now, I am giving various versions to you. Use it however you need: as a reference, a template, for a fill-in, or for students to copy.

Years after that first use, I went to an AVID workshop and learned about a three-level comprehension model published by a researcher named Stanovich in 1982. His levels were defined as 1, 2, and 3: "Read what is There, Read Between the Lines, and Read Beyond the Lines." Everytime I think of that, I am reminded that all research, all discovery about teaching unfolds first in our own classrooms.

Here, you'll find:
- A reference sheet to break down each column in my **three-level framework WN3D** and **two templates** for student use.

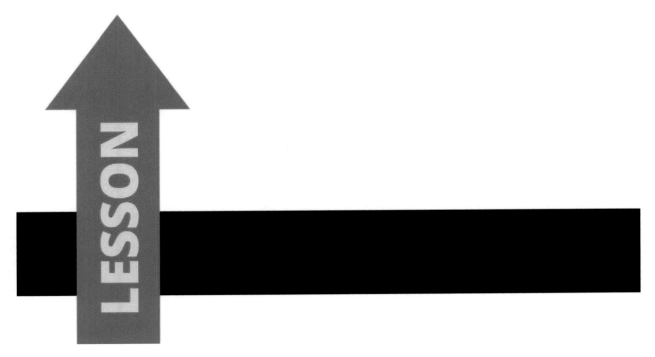

Williams' Note-Taking in 3D

Designed by Micole Williams

See literature from a **three-dimensional** standpoint!
In **three columns,** gather concrete and abstract details. After setting a **"fact" foundation,**
later build upon your notes and knowledge in order to
apply, analyze, synthesize and later evaluate
literature pieces **as a whole!**

Reading *the lines*	Reading *between the lines*	Reading *behind the lines*

(the **words**, the sentences, the structure of the sentences)	(**within** the plot points and setting, **literary elements** help to paint the **big picture)**	(facts about the **one who put the pen to paper)**
*syntax focus *rhyme scheme determination *technical devices used to group or break down the words or wording	characterization X conflict • style – metaphors, personification, similes, imagery, irony, etc ∆ symbols and meaning, O themes will be determined ? suspense or foreshadowing	* time period and date published * the background story of the author's influence * his/her intention * if the piece was not intended, how did the work come about

Each of the **three categories** have a **distinct purpose,** yet there are times **they may intertwine** in order to **determine the overall significance of the literature piece.** After applying these categories to your fact gathering process, you will have a concrete way of looking at abstract ideas in order to form research papers, portfolios, debates and critiques in the end!

Williams' Note-taking in 3D (each line is worth 4 points)

Title " _____ " by _____

Reading the lines (surface value/glance)	Reading between the lines (analysis) Recognized Devices you can quote and later explain the effect/benefit	Reading behind the lines (history/purpose)
Source/Publication: " _____ "	**-Aristotle's Appeals** (how the rhetor build ethos, pathos and/or logos) try to see examples of each... " _____ " " _____ " " _____ "	**The Rhetor:** brief bio in your own words
Genre: _____ **Format:Overall Organizational pattern** (problem-solution, cause-effect, compare-contrast, description, etc		**Exigence** – (significance of time period that influenced the piece)
	-Literary terms you need to always touch	**Rhetor's POV** due to time period
Navigating from Beginning, middle to end, determine syntactical structure- (sentence types: simple, compound, complex)	**-Tone** _____ **-Style** _____ **-Figurative language** (metaphors, similes, etc) " _____ "	**Author's purpose/duty:** _____
B: _____ **M:** _____ **E:** _____	**-Theme** _____ " _____ "	**Target audience:** _____
Topics and allusions: _____	***2 Open-ended questions you can answer** 1. _____ 2. _____	**Overall effect on the reader:** _____
Diction: (anaphora/motifs) " _____ "		

Williams' Note-Taking in 3D

See literature from a **three-dimensional** standpoint! In **three columns,** gather concrete and abstract details. After setting a **"fact" foundation, later build** upon your notes and knowledge in order to apply, analyze, synthesize and later evaluate literature pieces **as a whole!**

Reading *the lines*

(the **words**, the **sentences**, the **structure** of the sentences)

***syntax** focus determination
***rhyme scheme**
***technical devices** used to group or break down the words or wording

Reading *between the lines*

(**within** the plot points and setting, **literary elements** help to paint the **big picture**)
characterization

X conflict
* **style** – metaphors, personification, similes, imagery, irony, etc
Δ **symbols** and meaning,
O themes will be determined
? suspense or foreshadowing

Reading *behind the lines*

(facts about the **one who put the pen to paper**)

* time period and **date** published
* the **background story** of the author's **influence**
* his/her **intention**
* if the piece was not intended, how did the work come about

Each of the **three categories** have a **distinct purpose,** yet there are times **they may intertwine** in order to **determine the overall significance of the literature piece**. After applying these categories to your fact gathering process, you will have a concrete way of looking at abstract ideas in order to form research papers, portfolios, debates, and critiques in the end!

Make Colorful Sandwiches:
Color-Coded Sentences for Analytical Paragraphs

No matter the school, no matter the grade level, from one standardized test to another, from one classroom to the other, I had fun paying close attention to each school's preferred approach to strengthening students' analytical writing. One thing remained true: **To strengthen essays, one must first strengthen paragraphs. To strengthen paragraphs, one must strengthen sentences.**

According to *College Board's AP Vertical Teams Guide for English,* when examining author's style, students will find it useful to write a paragraph "that contains at least one sentence describing the author's syntax, one about his or her imagery and figurative language, one about the diction and one about symbolism and/or concrete details. This type of description is good practice for the Advanced Placement English Examinations" (42). The approach helps establish a common language for analysis.

I am a very visual person. I love talking in colors. The school I've taught at for over six years shares the same philosophy. So I use color-coded sentences for analytical paragraphs, self-assessment, and peer evaluation. AP Language students are not the only ones who benefit from such in-depth analysis. Color-coding helps on-level students as well.

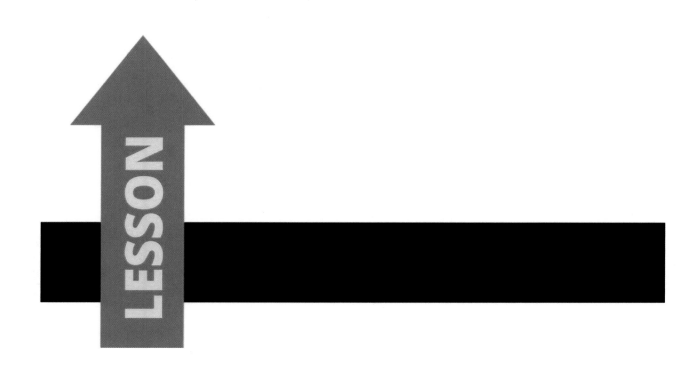

Make colorful sandwiches structuring analytical paragraphs

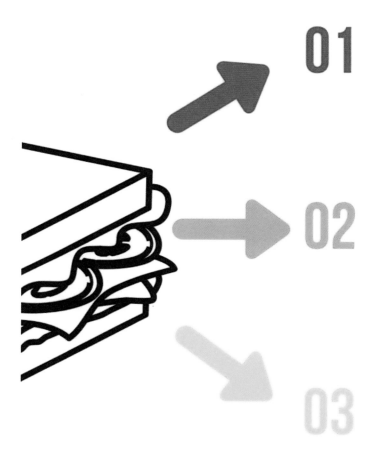

01 Analytical Claim

Answer/Address the prompt by creating a
- topic sentence or
- thesis statement

02 Evidence to Support Claim

It can come in the form of
- a poster child
- a current event
- historical event
- factual recall
- textual evidence

03 Your Insight on the Evidence

Explain the author's intent based on your

- interpretation

Make Colorful Sandwiches:

Color-Coded Sentences for Analytical Paragraphs

Choose one of the questions below.
Answer thoroughly with evidence from the text.

1. What is a dominant message expressed throughout the piece?
2. What two main subjects are displayed? How do they help determine the purpose of the piece?
3. What device or technique is effectively utilized by the author?
4. Who is the speaker? Who is the intended audience of the piece?
5. What is the significance of the occasion? How does it help determine the tone of the piece?

1

2

3

Inspiration for the World
Keep Finding It...

Find inspiration for the world. Do some research online. What pieces are inspirational compositions that can help our country's climate, morale, and spirit?

Below, copy and place the link of two pieces (one can be a song, another a poem or even an article) that share a similar theme. Make colorful sandwiches.

Copy and paste the link for selection 1
Copy and paste the link for selection 2
What do selection 1 and selection 2 have in common thematically? 1 2 3

Facilitate Literary Discussions:

"If you are shy, you won't be after this course." I love hearing my students' ideas about literature and the world around them. I encourage them to speak freely and to be aware of others' freedom. I also encourage them to agree to disagree in a civil manner, keeping decorum as they showcase their theories as global citizens. I have found that over time, students raise the standard and set higher expectations on their own.

In *Literature Circles: Voice and Choice in Book Clubs & Reading Groups*, Harvey Daniels explores two decades of the literature circle and its continued evolution. Five common steps rise again and again: 1. Explain, 2. Demonstrate, 3. Practice, 4. Debrief, 5. Refine (55).

Benefits	**Grading options**
- Students are responsible for facilitating - Promotes respectful and active collaboration and feedback - Evaluates a number of comprehension and communication skills	- 50/50 point scale for each timed round - Holistically measuring the quality and detail of answers and conversation, using a rubric
Things to think about Options are endless! - The driving open-ended questions can be prepared by the teacher or brought in by students - The stimulus can be prepared by the teacher or brought in by students	**Here you'll find** - My 9th - 12th grade students' favorite framework: the inner and outer circle - Directions for students - General literary questions or directives that can be used easily across texts

LESSON

Facilitate Book of Choice Discussions:
Inner and Outer Circles

Overview
1. A whole-class or choice-reading text will be assigned in advance.
2. Each class member will come to class with material they have prepared while pre-reading the selection in order to participate in the inner and outer circle rotations explained below.
3. Student leaders will emerge to facilitate and guide discussion. Students should initiate meaningful and quality discussion.
4. The teacher will not be in the conversation but may debrief between rotations if necessary.

The rotations are timed equally and are both worth 50 points.

Inner Circle Responsibilities: Talks. The discussion covers their own insight on the subject proposed. They can share their reflection, analysis, and question(s). They will need to be able to provide or refer back to evidence from the text that can further support their ideas. They should show active listening and engagement throughout.

Outer Circle Responsibilities: Listens/Observes. The outer circle listens. They should take notes over the inner circle's discussion and write down ideas and commentary. They provide the praise report for communicators that effectively answer questions in the inner circle. They are specific about how the communicator was effective. Outer circle members MUST NOT take part in the discussion!

Make sure to earn and not lose points.

Top 5 ways to earn points 1. Maintain a courteous composure. 2. Supply needed and interesting facts and proven or valid opinions. 3. Identify vague areas that may benefit from clarification and kindly elicit elaboration. 4. Validate others' thoughts and opinions by offering interpretation or connection and showing personal understanding. 5. Encourage others to share and aid in defusing conflict.

Top 5 ways to lose points 1. Refuse to participate in either circle's rotation. 2. Showcase disrespectful behavior (physical or verbal). 3. Display distracting nonverbal social cues. 4. Make counterproductive or off-task remarks. 5. Hog the conversation (while in the inner circle) or talk when you are to be listening (while in the outer circle).

Book of Choice Inner and Outer Circle
Discussion Questions

Part One - answer in a detailed paragraph about your fiction reading.

i.e. use Colorful Sandwiches or
Reporter's Formula: Who, What, When, Where, Why and How

1. Describe your reading experience.
2. What made you select this book?
3. This book made me feel_____.
4. Cast the main characters for the movie version.
5. Read your favorite quote and explain. Present your own open-ended question that was inspired by the quote.
6. Comment on one of the following: characters or author
7. Comment on language and tone.
8. Comment on one of the following: plot or structure.
9. Comment on one of the following: time period or theme.
10. Comment on one of the following: symbol or book cover.

Part Two

- answer in a detailed paragraph about your fiction reading.
i.e. use Colorful Sandwiches or
Reporter's Formula: Who, What, When, Where, Why and How

1. What is a good, alternative title?
2. What aspect, or part of a character, can you relate to and why?
3. What do you think inspired the author to write this book?
4. Who will this book impact? Who won't be interested?
5. What other story is like this one?
6. If this book was made into a movie, what technical details need to be emphasized?
7. What emoticon/emoji should symbolize your book?
8. What genre or sub category best describes your book?
9. If you had to rewrite this piece, what would and wouldn't you change?
10. What rating, on a scale from 1-5, would you rate the book?

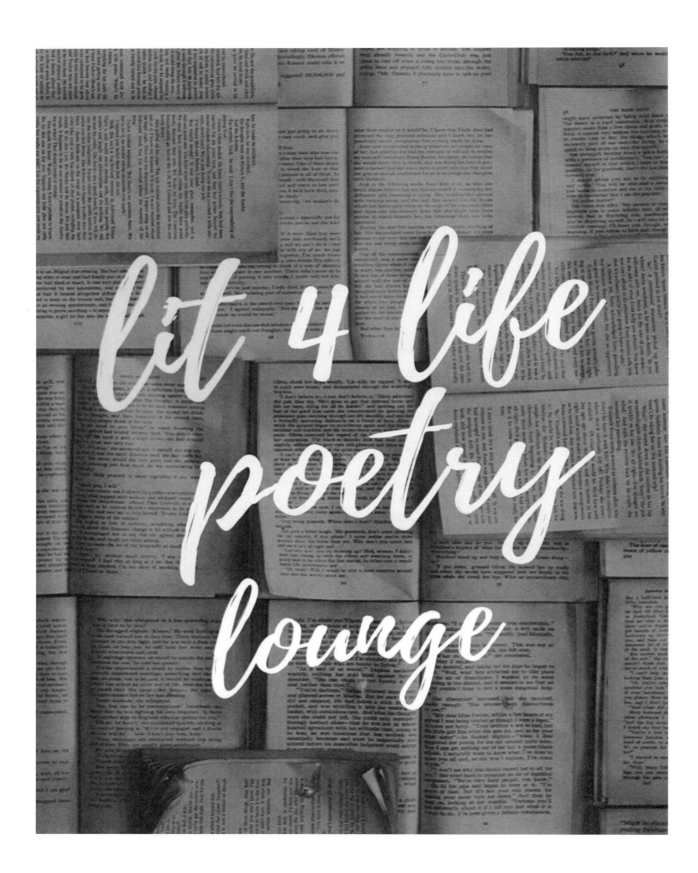

lit 4 life
poetry
lounge

Poetry Lounge

This section is a *little* different. I didn't want to forget poetry. I attended an ABYDOS Institute in 2014, and we worked out of the *ACTS of Teaching* book. It says, "Students working with poetry are like a well. Water comes flowing forth or the well is clogged and dry." It also brings up the reality that "difficulty arises with what students do with the poem after they write one" (49). My personal takeaway is that students learn more by examining poetry outside of themselves to enhance their own poems. In this extension, you will find activities I've crafted for my students that call for analysis in order to create.

Analysis - Create - Analysis : Aside from using poems in the class for analysis, it is great to remember the spoken aspect of poetry in order to keep things current. After analysis, I have students create impromptu pieces that they can present live. The end result is a class poetry lounge where these words can be shared. In this lounge, students can analyze each other's pieces, as well as appreciate them.

Here you'll find:

1. **Poetic Interpretation:** a quick activity that can serve as a hook

2. **Poetry Talk: a set of discussion questions** that can serve as a diagnostic, review, or sectioned activity when paired with poems you want your class to analyze. The questions allow you to address many different types of poetry, how to measure this artform, and even how to evaluate great poetry.

3. **Picture to Poem**: **Steps to a 5-Part Mini-Lesson** that gets students looking at poetry differently. These scaffolded steps reveal how photographic memories can serve as muses for their own poetry. I walk students through this discovery brainstorm and pre-write as they analyze details that will soon unfold into a poem. There are some additional items for students to incorporate into their prewrite.

4. **Teacher Model:** This is the sample I used for my students: it includes my picture, my prewrite, and my poem.

5. **WN3D with Poetry:** This handout can be used to record analysis of assigned, student-selected, or even original poems read in the lit-for-life poetry lounge. WND3 can be used with poetry throughout the unit.

Host a Lit for Life Lounge: Poetry and Prose

One of my favorite pastimes is visiting spoken-word poetry lounges in the city. Bringing this element to the class is always fun. Students love having their moment to shine and instant feedback. Some of the best original work comes from challenges like this because it is the core of who they are on display.

1. I change the lighting a bit and create a stage for students to read their poetry.
2. I play hip-hop, jazz music in the background as they walk in.
3. I go over house rules.
4. After each poet, the snaps and key-shaking keeps coming!

Here, you'll find:

1. A **warm-up**
2. Poetry Talk **Questions**
3. **Picture-to-Poem** Activity (Poem /Prewrite)
4. **Teacher Model - Prewrite**
5. **Teacher Model - Poem**

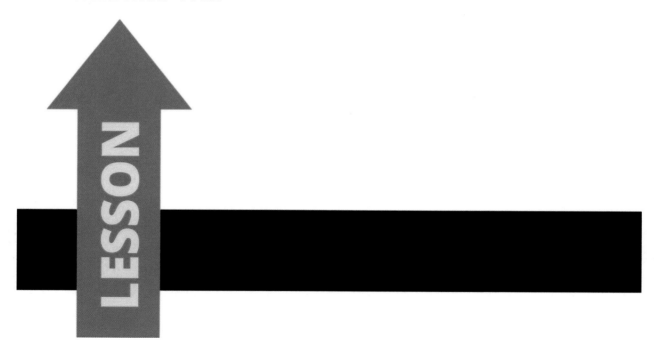

LESSON

Poetic Interpretation
Close your eyes. Listen.
What do you see when I read this?
Draw it...

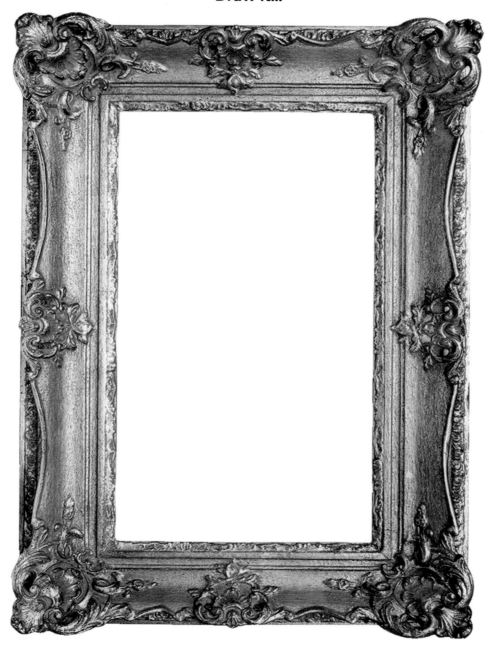

Poetry Talk

I. What are the different types of poetry?
   - What are the functions and characteristics of these types of poems? **(i.e. free verse, haiku, narrative, concrete, lyrical, and sonnets)**

II. What are various elements of poetry?
   - How does sensory language affect the reader's experience of the text?
   - How do poets use imagery to convey meaning?
   - What are some nuances you have found in poetry?
   - How did the poet use poetic techniques to create meaning?
   - What conclusions can you draw about the intended tone of the piece?
   - What are the advantages of using allusion instead of literal wording?
   - What is the difference between poetry and prose?

III. How can you determine the meter of a poem?
   - What effect does the meter of a poem have on its meaning?
   - How can you label the rhyme schemes ?
   - What effect does rhyme (all or specified types) have on the overall audience?

IV. How does society affect poetry? How does poetry affect society?
   - Which piece of evidence most appropriately supports the question/meaning?
   - What modern-day article connects to this poem?

Picture to Poem

Part one
Find a photo (on your phone or at home) that represents
the essence of who you are.

Part two
Create a two-columned chart.
Label the left column: the concrete
Label the right column: the abstract

Part three
Study the photo and list 5 concrete items you or others
can touch or see on/in the picture.

Part four
Now add meaning to the items. What does each item represent?

Part five
Write your own poem, letting the picture serve as your muse.
Effectively incorporate elements below.

CHECKLIST
_____5 examples of imagery (concrete transitions into meaning) (50 points)

_____Taste (sensory detail) (10 points)

_____Smell (sensory detail) (10 points)

_____Simile included (10 points)

_____Clear TONE/THEME/MOOD (10 points)

_____Symbolic title (10 points)

Teacher Model
Stairsteps
By Micole Williams

CONCRETE: *What I CAN TOUCH OR SEE*	ABSTRACT: *What I CAN FEEL OR EXPERIENCE*
1. stairsteps	a place where generations sit, passing down wisdom in order to build innovation
2. stage	a place where the family can present the best of life and the worst of life - applause and Kleenex
3. smiles	the prelude to the proliferating synthesis of laughter showcasing compassion and love that stands the test of time
4. stair-railing	**like** a memory, something secure and sturdy enough to hold on to
5. turkey	The sweet **smell** of the holiday that brings together those who live far apart, but those who are close in heart, the **taste** of Thanksgiving is so delicious.

**stairsteps
by
micole
williams**

**We sit
on
stairsteps,**

**a place where
generations pass down
wisdom in order to build
innovation. The stair-rail,
like a memory, it is something secure
and sturdy enough to hold on to.
We await the show. The stage is a
place where the family can present
the best of life and the worst of life
- applause and Kleenex follow.**

**While sharing the latest news, smiles stretch
across faces - the prelude to the proliferating
synthesis of laughter showcasing compassion
and love that stands the test of time.
Finally the turkey is ready! The sweet smell of the
holiday brings together those who live far apart,
but those who are close in heart.
The taste of Thanksgiving is soooo delicious!**

WN3D with Poetry

Review the poem. Pay attention to literal and figurative details and how they interrelate with the bigger picture. Below, note succinct observations and analysis of format, meaning, and intent in order to establish relevance and meaning.

Reading the lines	Reading between the lines	Reading behind the lines
Diction	**Theme**	**Exigence – time period**
	Tone	
	Figurative language	**Author's style**
Syntax		
	***Open-ended questions** 1.	
		Author's purpose
Format techniques		
	2.	
Organization		

ART
ANALYSIS

FREE ADMISSION

Appreciate Art in ELA: Take "In-Class" Field Trips to the Museum

Art truly helps promote creativity and analysis. Like the old saying goes, a picture is worth a thousand words. Therefore, art is an unending way to cover analysis and get students to openly share their interpretation of a piece.

Like poetry lounges, going to the museum is also a hobby of mine. In 2017, I checked out these #slowart exercises at the Museum of Fine Arts - Houston, and that gave me inspiration for a new class assignment that proved to be a nice break in the routine, considering how closely we deal with the written word.

This section is also a bit different.

What you'll find:

I have pre-made charts that students can either write on or use to duplicate on lined paper. The **two-part graphic organizers** will take them through a scaffolded process of analyzing diverse artworks so they can have their own ELA version of #slowart.

1. **ELA Art Chart Part One -** Record detailed examination of the aesthetics, elements, and choices made by the artist. Predict the work's possible meaning or intent.
2. **ELA Art Chart Part Two -** Once the artist's intent or art history is revealed, students apply facts and record evidence in the appropriate place to reinforce, enlighten, or challenge earlier ideas
3. **ELA Art Exit Ticket -** Students prove their understanding by focusing on one of the smaller parts of the big picture.

Steps for the Teacher "Curator"

1. Serving as a curator for the day, visit four distinct pieces of art that are researched and a part of the class collection. Give the overview of the day.
2. **For ELA Art Chart Part One -** Build in quiet time for students to determine answers without interruptions or sidetalk.
3. Segue into revisiting details as a whole group. Discuss details and later what these observations could mean. Encourage various points of view.
4. **Assign homework -** Students create a fictional or nonfictional story based on the details they recorded and interpreted.
5. The next day, reveal facts about the picture. These details need to be recorded to complete **ELA Art Chart Part Two. Debrief about discoveries.**

ELA Art Chart

Title of the piece:

Artist:

PART ONE: First, examine the piece and record what you notice. Then add meaning to your observations. Later, share your thoughts and interpretation.

What I see...	What it could mean...
Consider shapes	
Consider color	
Consider objects or subjects	

ELA Art Chart

PART TWO: Using the background information and history provided, determine the appropriate answers below.

Piece # Title Artist	
What are 3 pertinent facts or details about the piece?	
This piece means...	
This piece matters to...	
What is significant about the time period and the artist?	

ELA Art

Choose an exit ticket and post your answer.

1. Explain how one of the pieces is ironic.

2. Explain how one of the pieces is ambiguous.

3. Explain how one piece showcases a biblical/historical or literary allusion.

4. Rename each piece. Create an original title that could also be appropriate.

5. Compare each piece with a modern-day piece of art (art being artform).

STORY CENTRAL

DEAR TEACHER,

Celebrating various cultures in the classroom is a powerful choice. It establishes the idea that each of our own personal stories matters. From the beginning to the middle to the end of the school year, I believe in finding ways to explore what makes us *who we were, are, and strive to be*. Focusing on culture helps us all become more aware of our individuality and connectivity. It also helps us to embrace and appreciate diversity in thought, action, and expression. Finding links to diverse stories that are rich in culture serve us greatly in a multitude of ways.

Here are some ways that have worked for my class.

1. At the beginning of the year, creating a **culture quilt** (a linked set of index cards that detail each student's culture) is a powerful activity that unifies and celebrates diversity.
2. In the middle of the year, the students see a **different side** of me. Normally, I am pretty mature, but I let them into **my world** of holiday celebration. I surprise them when they walk in with impromptu instructions that normally send them into a frenzy: Dance down the *Soul Train* line to my favorite Christmas song.
3. At the end of the year, allowing students to share **"send-off notes"** to their classmates is a powerful and thoughtful way to wrap up the year.
4. Build a **classroom library** of new trending books and solid classics for students to borrow from and add to. School librarians and department leaders can often help with this.

SCRIPTURE

"Declaring the end from the beginning, And from ancient times things which have not been done, Saying, 'My purpose will be established, and I will accomplish all my good pleasure."
Isaiah 46:10

INSPIRATION

"Narrative is radical, creating us at the very moment it is created."
Toni Morrison

Everyone has a story*...* **personally, culturally, historically, and currently. Various pieces can showcase literary techniques that help shape a narrative that speaks to the human condition.**

Studies continue to prove that reading fiction increases not only empathy, but inspiration for writing. "Books can make the difference. They can make classrooms bristle with meaning ... shared books can create a world for writing" (Calkins, 22). Drama as a genre and core element has a similar effect. I think of Stanislavski's "Magic If": When we read and perform, we can embody another character for that time and place. Stories are powerful. They can open the door to needed dialogue, thoughtful self-reflection, and transformative revelation. Pick wisely!

Here, you'll find:
- **Materials** that allow students to respond and showcase understanding of their book of choice or the model text
- **Prompts** for students to create their own stories in the form of fiction or drama

Let's let the stories unfold!

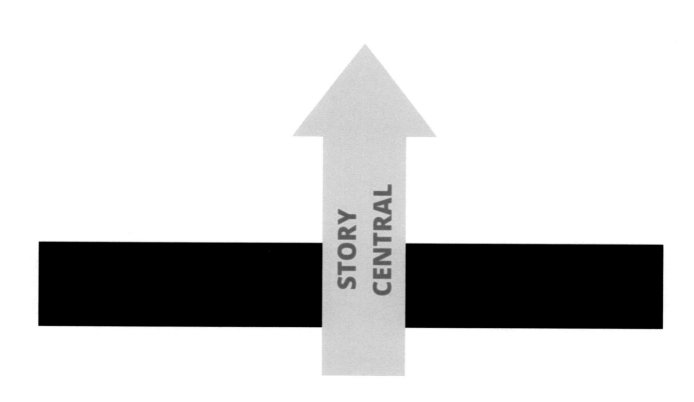

STORY CENTRAL

Story Central

+ Make a Lit-For-Life Foldable
(A Crafty Resource and Assessment)

+ Hunt for Lit Elements Scavenger Hunt
(Enrichment Reading Activity)

+ Team Up for Flash Fiction
(Flex Fiction Writing Muscles)

+ Read Closely / Make Annotations
(Dialectical Responses)

+ Review Others' Stories
(Write a Movie Review)

+ Reimagine Others' Stories
(Make a Production Poster / Recast a Play)

... at my current school, preparing the campus Writer's Showcase and my students' flash fiction pieces ...

LIT FOR LIFE

FICTION

EXPLORERS

wheres
your
road?

Make a Lit-For-Life Foldable

I like getting crafty and colorful - *even with high school students.* I've come to realize they like this too. Early in the year, this is another year-round resource that students are to create, customize, and keep in their binders. They are expected to add details to this foldable and refer to them during a variety of activities. The foldable is a compact place where students can store tons of valuable information they will need throughout the year.

Preparation	Directions for the crafty session
- Teacher model of the finished product - Model cards placed around the classroom contain definitions and examples to each of the tab's titles.	- Students pick 5 sheets of colorful printer paper and spread them out evenly so that it is easy to fold and staple.
Class set up - Supply station where students can select colorful sheets - Set up as a gallery walk or stations - Time reminders - Phones can be used to take pics of those missed due to time	**Focus Points** - Nuanced concepts or ones commonly confused with each other - Extra info important to their grade level (such as customized scoring for their end-of-year standardized test or even more literary terms that they should not forget)

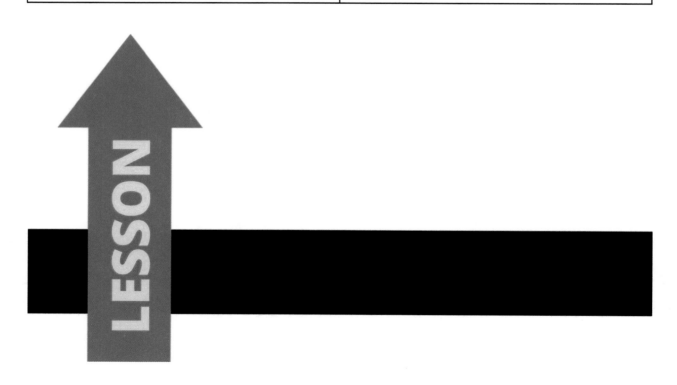

...A Crafty Resource

Teacher Model...

Take the Lit-for-Life Quiz

Stressing that note-taking and copying of notes is a simple task, I like to see if students are retaining the notes that are copied.

When students have completed their foldable, in order to ensure that students took meaningful notes initially and are retaining the information, the next day they are to complete a timed quiz covering some of what I call phase one.

Sometimes I let them use their foldable for a portion of the time as a lifeline. Decide what is best for your group and their level.

Here you'll find:

- A **quiz** that follows the creation of the **Lit-for-Life** foldable
- Teacher **answer key**

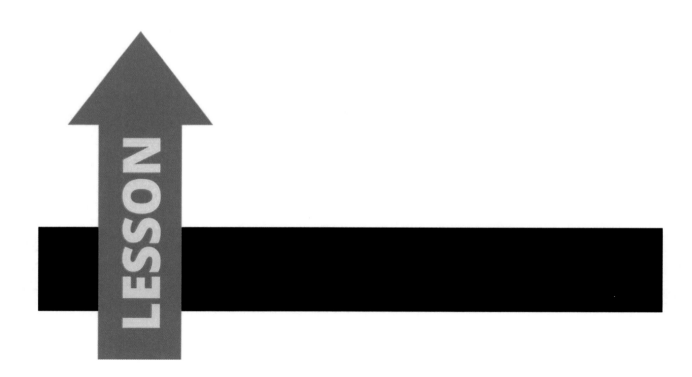

Take the LIT For Life Quiz

10 minute limit

Write the correct answer for each example provided.
Foldables can be used as a last resort.

1. _____how one can structure sentences
2. _____the author's attitude toward a subject
3. _____the central message of a story
4. _____appealing to the 5 senses
5. _____definition from the dictionary
6. _____essay with a one-sided argument
7. _____distinctive sound of the author / their way of speaking
8. _____definition created from emotional association
9. _____the controlling idea
10. _____author's choice of words

TEACHER KEY
1. syntax
2. tone
3. theme
4. imagery
5. denotation
6. persuasive essay
7. voice
8. connotation
9. thesis statement
10. diction

Hunt for Lit Elements

Managing independent reading is a struggle, isn't it? Here are my two biggest struggles:

1. We cannot simply read for pure enjoyment every day.
2. It's also not every day that we read what we want.

Well those, and this: How can you determine if a student is actually reading?

We have to have a standard for assessing the quality of so many students' varied reading experiences. I wanted to create something that would allow students to:
1. Choose their own book,
2. Actually engage with the text, and
3. Allow me to witness and evaluate in real-time (or later).

Since I love games, this is a timed hunt for evidence of literary elements in a student's fiction novel. I would try to work in this type of reading at least once a month. Before the hunt for *lit* elements begins, let students define the elements they are not familiar with and store definitions in their foldable.

The GLOSSARY in this book may help.

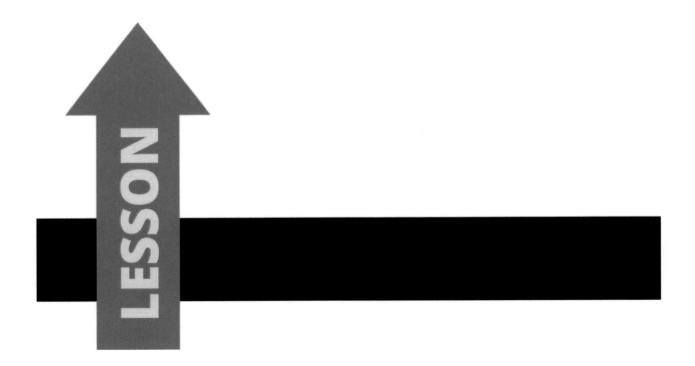

LIT SCAVENGER HUNT

On your own sheet of paper, you are to log appropriate literary term examples you have observed during your reading experience.

PART I. THE HUNT - **Silently, read your "Book of Choice" in class during the uninterrupted time limit to understand the premise of the story.**
Notice what your author is doing with figurative language and sensory details to enhance the reading experience.

---

*Allusion *Foreshadowing *Juxtaposition *Paradox *5 Sensory Details *Alliteration *Hyperbole *Jargon *Personification *Simile *Anaphora* Imagery* Metaphor *Pun *Symbolism *Characterization *Irony *Motif *Rhetorical Question *Theme *Conflict (specify type) *Idiom *Onomatopoeia

*Add Your Own

_____

PART II. THE CAPTURE - **Document** examples of meaningful and/or dominant literary language that you are noticing during your reading or skimming. Capture the amount you need to earn the grade you want before time is up. Follow the format below.

EACH QUOTE WILL BE WORTH 10 Points. Each term or example can only be used once and must be correct to earn full points. Follow the **FORMAT** below to avoid point deductions.

Heading your paper like this:

Book Bevery Moody Takes on America Author Fran Sage Rd pgs from 30 to 50

Number and LOG LITERARY
EXAMPLES like this:

NOTE: You can use ellipses to narrow your quote down to what is really needed.

1. *Literary Term personification Page 52*

   Quote "...the sun decided to leap and dance in the air."

Team Up For Flash Fiction

As teachers, we are queens and kings of improvising. When the lights go out due to storms, my windowless room gets super dark, and I have to think fast. Who wants 30 teens in the dark for any length of time? *Hey! It's time to test out our campfire skills.* I'd get out the flashlight. *It's story time!*

I like when students come together to tell stories.

Sometimes, after so much reading and analyzing, one just needs to be creative. There's also something special about ingenuity. Our imaginative mind should be valued and exercised right along with analytical thinking.

This brings me to one of my favorite activities: flash fiction. Normally, after a long year and testing, I assign flash fiction to give the mind a brain break. Through this, I have found some of the best writing from students. I had the pleasure of organizing the school's ELA Writer's Showcase these past two years. All ELA students' work was on display. A showcase is a great opportunity to test out Flash Fiction and other original expressions.

Here you'll find:
- A **plot map graphic organizer** for students to organize key points in the story
- The two-in-one: **project details and template**

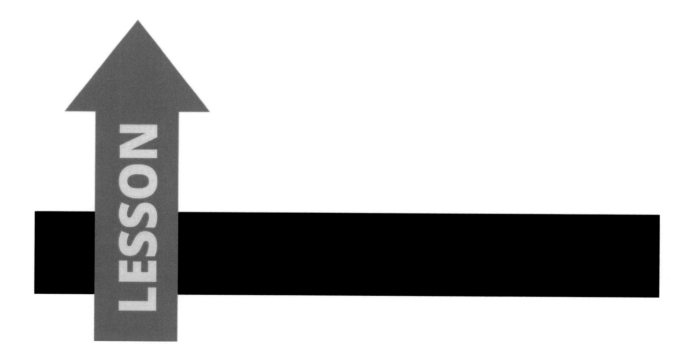

LESSON

FLASH FICTION CHALLENGE Prewrite

What is possible for your story? Write what will happen at each plot point.

Plot Diagram

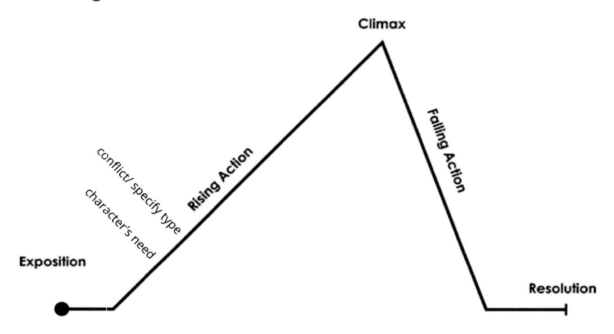

FLASH FICTION CHALLENGE

Each box represents a page either in example or directions.

In small groups and in a timed setting,
create a one-page fiction story that includes 5 plot points:

Cover page (instructions and sample below) Create the elements below. Look at the sample for further help. **10 points each** 1. Create a symbolic **title** 2. Create a subtitle that reveals the **theme** which is the message/moral of the story 3. Copy and paste a **picture**. Photo caption the picture with the closest thing to the photographer or the one who gives permission for use. You can also put "courtesy of ____" 4. For the teaser, share the author's purpose. Write one sentence to tell why it was created. Use a vivid verb. 5. Add names of members and *Flash Fiction Short Story Collection* at the very bottom of your page.	**Story (instructions and sample below) **50 points total**** Type a complete, error-free final draft that showcases 5 plot points and evidence of response to notes/suggestions and feedback from the teacher. The story should fit on ONE PAGE. You may have to adjust the font, the size, and the spacing of lines for an audience to read comfortably while it is on display. I will also print out a booklet with all copies, so do present your best work. Points will be deducted if there are mistakes in -spelling -capitalization -punctuation -grammar, etc.
  # Vacancy ...a haunting tale about a house that is not a home  **(Photo by KTRK) (8 point font)** *by* *Maya Giovanni, Nikki Angelou Micoley Cole, and King Stephen* *This story illustrates how buried secrets can live to haunt you...* *2020 Williams' Flash Fiction Short Story Collection*	*THE WHOLE, ONE - PAGE STORY,* *YOUR FLESHED OUT DETAILS, SHOULD GO HERE*

Read Closely /Make Annotations (Dialectical Responses)

I believe that the text is foundation, and we need to inspect it. We need to make observations, and the only way to do that is to get up close. We have to walk the exterior and interior, survey it for creepy crawlers, make sure the pipes are in good shape, and evaluate the small details that determine the overall condition. In *Notice & Note: Strategies for Close Reading,* Beers and Probst put it like this : "To ignore either element in the transaction, to deny the presence of the reader or neglect the contribution of the text, is to make reading impossible" (36).

As an educator, I have found that it takes observation, processing control, execution, and skill to keep a classroom going. Those same things apply to dialectical journals. These customized entries are a great way for students to find value in their own reading experience by interacting with the text and later with their peers. This strategy has proven to be a great way to gauge a student's reading process. The journals can be created and shared online for continuous dialogue.

Here you'll find:
1. An **annotations guide sheet** for students that lists types of observations and thoughts that can be noted while reading
2. A **graphic organizer** that serves as a segue into **dialectical journals**
3. A **colorful sandwiches** extension activity with **four close-reading questions**

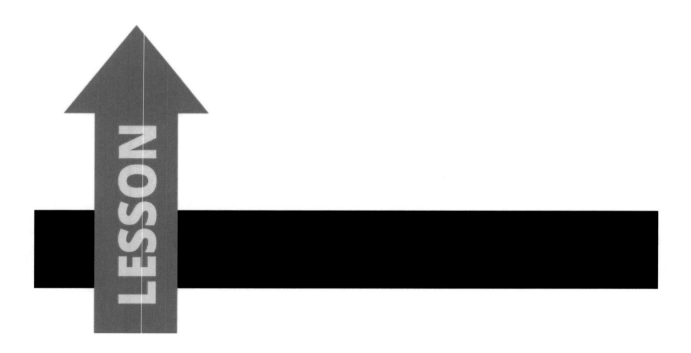

Make Annotations

1. How is marking the text different from making annotations?
2. Annotations are notes that are written in the form of (name all that apply).

First read "for the what". Second read for "the how" and "the why".

Be able to:
1. **Mark your text** with appropriate labels where you can find evidence.
2. **Annotate** by writing meaningful statements and observations beside the appropriate label. Showcase meaningful analysis. *How* do the devices/techniques or literary techniques add meaning to this piece? *Why* is this appeal being employed? What is to be learned? What is the moral to this story? Be prepared to present ideas in small group discussions.

Annotation Analysis Options (labels to mark on text are bolded)

Personal Links What are you able to relate to and why? What are your feelings about these associations?

Main Idea Locate the thesis and put a star by it. Label any supporting details MI.

Plot Connection How is this piece similar to another text or concept?

Theme What does this piece mean? What universal truth is displayed?

Lit Evidence Name the **device/technique/term** you see. Explain the author's intent.

Style How is the author using language in a unique way? What is the author's distinctive sound?

Characterization What are meaningful inner and outer details of a character or subject? How do they drive the plot or add purpose to the piece?

Voice What types are presented? What do they each represent? How do they interact with one another?

Geography What personal, local, national, and/or global details help build a distinctive world?

Structure How are shifts or patterns displayed?

Appeals What are examples of effective use of pathos, logos or ethos? Are there ineffective logical fallacies?

Question What confuses you or fails to be answered due to the author's intent or lack of clarity?

Prediction Through clues, what is being foreshadowed?

Answers What has been revealed to answer earlier questions and predictions?

Dialectical Responses

Journal Entry #___

Textual Evidence - Select a quote from your reading.	Page # Paragraph #	Label and Response: Carry over the labels from annotations - Explain the significance of this quote with your analysis and insight.

Read Closely

Answer in colorful sandwiches. Think about what the passage or text is suggesting. Think about what is revealed about the characters. Write a thoroughly developed paragraph explaining how the author develops ideas in a thoughtful way. Be sure to use textual evidence to prove your answer. Use your annotations to develop thoughtful responses or insightful observations and discoveries.

1. Based on the main idea and supporting details, what is one possible theme of the piece?

2. Factoring in what is presented about the environment, how does imagery illustrate the speaker's outer world?

3. Determine aspects of the character's or subject's internal motivation and struggle. How does characterization reflect the speaker's inner world and conflict?

4. What is the tone of the piece? How is it used to determine purpose?

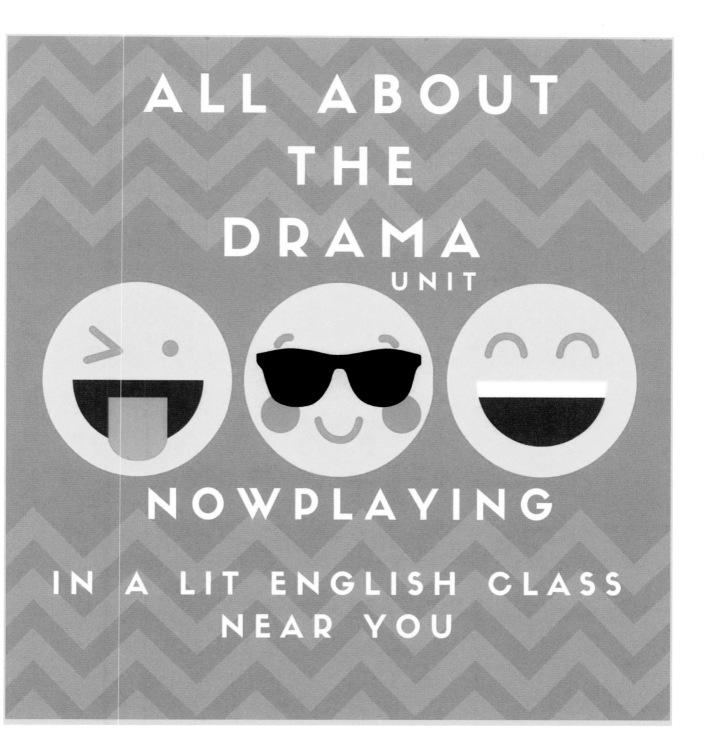

All About the Drama

I had to throw some drama in the mix. What's a story without it, right? It definitely spices things up and makes students see another side to the written word and themselves. "Students cannot be totally independent and self-sufficient while working with drama. Not only does drama insist on collaboration but also it exercises imaginative muscles" (Carrol, Wilson, 49). It's always great to see the thespians come out in the ELA room. I assign challenges for students to recreate and even rewrite scenes from plays they've just completed for their peers to watch live or as video.

You will find two assignments that work well in your drama unit or visual/media arts component. Whether you are reading excerpts or full plays, or watching clips or a full movie after reading the book, there is something here for you.

Here, you'll find:

1. **Movie Tie-in** - writing assignment

2. **Stage Play Tie-in** - design assignment

Review Others' Stories

Critics come in all shapes and sizes. They can also come from the classroom. It's never easy to be on the receiving end of criticism. Being observed and critiqued can be taxing for any human being, even if it is constructive. But when delivered discerningly and thoughtfully, our substantiated opinions can shape the world we live in by influencing people one way or another. We need critics in order to improve and grow. We need critics in order to build greater character. We need critical thinkers in the classroom.

Students always wonder when they will use ELA in the "real world". Well, the blend of argument and expository writing has its place when factoring in writing that is helpful in any profession. Regarding the urgency of teaching expository argument, Michael Degan writes, many teachers "assign a 'five-paragraph essay' without providing students instruction in the composing process." Yet, "ensuring that students can write cogent, concise, and coherent exposition" should be an urgent focus at the secondary level (11). Being a movie buff, I used to review movies for different publications. This assignment came from the spirit of that professional experience. Of course, I made adjustments and outlined options for a common framework for persuasive or expository or a mixture of those genres.

Here, you'll find:
1. A **pre-writing template for a movie review** with a prompt and above outlining options of persuasive or expository
2. A **teacher model/frame** with built-in questions, directions, and my take on a popular and relevant young adult book-to-film project I knew students were talking about. Though I share my model before students start writing, I give them leeway to determine their own movie and, of course, their own style of writing (as long as they address the prompt).

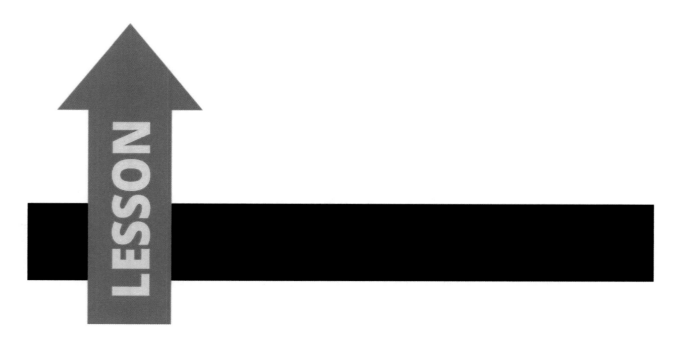

Write a Movie Review

PROMPT

Maintaining a neutral or persuasive position, compose a movie review, using the 5 elements of expository or persuasive writing/structure. Explore theme and execution of visual and audio elements to determine audience.

Outline

Persuasive Elements	Expository Elements
I. Hook II. Thesis III. Support 1 + Support 2 IV. Concession and Refutation V. Call to Action	I. Hook II. Thesis III. Support 1 IV. Support 2 V. Conclusion

I. _____

_____

_____

II. _____

_____

_____

_____

III. _____

_____

_____

_____

IV. _____

_____

_____

_____

V. _____

Teacher Model Movie Review of *"The Hate U Give"* by Micole Williams

PROMPT - Maintaining a neutral or persuasive position, compose a movie review, using the 5 elements of expository or persuasive writing/structure, and explore theme and execution of visual and audio elements to determine audience.

Hook: Share a personal anecdote that relates to the movie

Battles are around the corner. We all have them to face. Like the infamous words of Sophia in *The Color Purple*, "All my life I had to fight." Whether it be stereotypes or unethical and unfair practices, there is a battle. I remember fighting for my right to vote (*in the 21st century*). When I was a college student living in a rural community, many felt that though we occupied space in the community during our time in college, our voices should not count in a judicial way. We knew otherwise, and in record numbers we were going to stand for our beliefs. Feeling as though we were not heard, we were going to make a statement where it counted: On the steps of Waller County's City Hall. Peacefully, we marched, with and without signs, for miles, and we were not leaving the issue until we knew justice was ours. A recent movie made me a bit nostalgic. Holding my breath, fighting tears, and empathizing with anger, I watched this movie, knowing that a few times in life, during a few battles, I have felt the pain of feeling wronged and not vindicated. As I watched a teen endure far more harsh realities than I encountered in high school, I knew I was watching a film that will be talked about for many years to come. Here's why.

Thesis (make sure the theme is stated - write in present tense from this point on)

Produced with passion, this poignant tale, based on an award-winning novel, displays how the **fight for justice** is never a straight and narrow path, but a turbulent, unpredictable rollercoaster.

Support 1 What are the strengths and weaknesses of how the theme (the message of the story/ the moral) is carried out from the beginning, middle, and to the end?

The film, early on, gets to the heart of the matter: Exploring **pressing issues that riddle and ruin communities**. The film highlights a young lady who regretfully, yet dutifully, lives two lives. After witnessing the premature death of her dear friend and crush, Starr, the heroine, is hit with the question of how she can help **bring justice to an unjust situation?** She **struggles with the idea of truth** and how it does not always set one free, but it can oftentimes, in her neighborhood, gridlock you due to street codes and the "anti-snitch culture". The exigency of this film hits close to home, as many of us witness on the news and in many neighborhoods across the nation, a similar nightmare. The theme is carried out as she contemplates the best way to bring justice to Khalil who died due to assumptions rather than fact, at the hands of a policeman. _____. In the end, _____.

The film is realistic in how it illustrates, as Marvin puts it, "trigger-happy policing"—a growing epidemic. This movie showcases some parallels of how communities have had to rise up to fight for justice for the dead: the Travyon Martins, Sandra Blands, and the list goes on. What it does well is show a personal account of what a friend would encounter in this type of tragic event: What *we* could or have experienced. It also responsibly shows various sides of who this scenario affects; Starr's uncle, Carlos, is a policeman and brings in the voice of how officers can be victims too. Where it falls flat is the constant trauma. It does not let up. The whole movie is a climax. Be prepared to be on an emotional rollercoaster. Though I am sure it is intentional, and it does help bring about the reality factor that cannot be ignored, there is no relief period and some aspects at the end are_____.

Support 2: What are the strengths and weaknesses of carrying out the technical side? Speak on the execution of the film (how the director brings the story to life through audio and visual elements).

Having read some of the book, prior to seeing the movie, helped to form a picture in my head. Many aspects of the narrative are carried out verbatim. _____ The quality of the movie is _____ . The style of shooting is very clean and standard. There is not a lot of Spike Lee cinematography. Chances are not taken there, yet the images and music still produce a lot of emotion. It feels up-close-and-personal due to the choices in close ups on Starr's face at pivotal times, such as _____. The use of slow-motion is also helpful and very _____ and brings in an element of _____. Stunts and action were realistic _____. The _____ are _____. The music confused me a bit because I wondered what exact period of time is being captured. What is very clear are the two worlds Starr exists in. The choices in clothing help to showcase the two realities Starr has to juggle: The school that she attends is stark white and the neighborhood she lives in is earth-toned. The shots associated with the school, classmates' homes, and cars are wide and elaborate. For her home and neighborhood, the shots are tight and cluttered. She wears starched, preppy uniforms at her school and is the only speck of color in the halls. In her neighborhood, she sports baggy clothes and still stands out like a sore thumb because she is the talk of the town, being that she is one of the few going to a school outside of the neighborhood, and one that intimidates her friends. The film points out how she speaks and moves differently in both places. _____ . Overall, the movie successfully executes a juxtaposed life through simple, yet clear visuals and distinctly different sounds of both worlds. Showcasing the trickiness of "code-switching" helps form a bigger idea; it helps to shine a light on the fight that many young people endure while battling to establish their own identity in a big world that often does not make a lot of sense.

Conclusion - In a sentence or two, share who would not like the movie and who is this movie for.

Reimagine Others' Stories

After reading and even watching a clip of the adaptation of a play previously read in class, I think it is always interesting to wrap up a unit by allowing students to present *another* take, their own version of an existing classic. Giving a modern rendition to a classic is always a focus for me since it allows it to be relevant to them and validates their perception.

In the form of a theatrical stage play poster or Playbill, students can add their own personal touch on who they would like to bring this play to life now while showcasing media literacy and design skills.

I pick a few to make into a poster and display them outside of my classroom. This adds a great touch to the walls and helps to paint a theatrical mood.

Here, you'll find:
1. Directions for creating a **promo poster for a theatrical production**

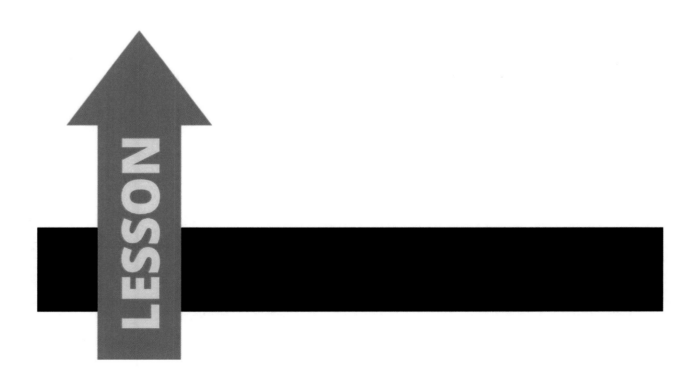

LESSON

Make A Production Poster / Recast the Play

Making sure all details are presented in clear, presentable form, create a production poster. Each element below is worth "10 points". Earn as many points as possible. Make the original writer proud and carry on a tradition with your own original rendition! Upload your complete movie poster as a document or PDF by deadline. The strongest samples will be blown up poster-size and displayed out in the hall.

Include:

_____**1. Title and writer of the production**

_____**2. List 5 main characters' names**

_____**3. 5 Actors/actresses names who will be cast as the characters/ (connect 2-3 in a presentable and clean way)**

_____**4. Determine tone and genre written, but write it as a statement and italicize it or enclose in quotation marks - quote/cite it as someone special (like a critic):**
ex. "a nostalgically vivid bio pic" - Parker Reviews

_____**5. Director's Name (you) and your fictional company.**

_____**6. Theme ex. "The future has a hand on you"**

_____**7. Release date - has to be this year**

_____**8. A significant illustration/ symbol or setting scene - this is somewhere on the page or as the background**

_____**9. Professionally Designed layout (use Canva.com or other design software to achieve the look)**

_____**10. No errors in spelling, capitalization, grammar, spacing**

PERSUASIVE PARKWAY

DEAR TEACHER,

Passion and persuasion go hand in hand. Since persuasion is a great tool for social change, there are many layers to its power. Persuasion is a process. It needs careful unpacking.

Here is where opinions matter, and if packaged and presented well, they can play a part in influencing people one way or another. Persuasive content is all around us, and there are many effectively used examples in society that I like to bring into the classroom.

Here are some ways we are moved by the art of persuasion:

- Advertisements
- PSAs
- Elevator Pitches
- Pop Culture Content
- Acceptance Speeches
- Campaigns
- Critics' Reviews

For AP students, books like *Thank You For Arguing* (Jay Heinrichs) and *Everything's an Argument* (Lunsford and Ruszkiewicz) not only define appeals and logical fallacies, but delve deeper into rhetoric and terminology that will be helpful for AP students.

For On-Level students, providing the breakdown of characteristics of the three appeals should work wonders.

SELF CARE

SCRIPTURE

"But above all, my brothers, do not swear, either by heaven or by earth or by any other oath, but let your "yes" be yes and your "no" be no, so that you may not fall under condemnation."
James 5:12

INSPIRATION

"Character may almost be called the most effective means of persuasion."
Aristotle

Everything's an argument...

Me: *Everything* is an argument. If you don't agree with this statement, please raise your hand.

(There is always one student who raises his or her hand.)

Me: Point Proven

(A few students laugh, getting the point.)

I love persuasion. It comes in handy. Even as teachers, in order to do our jobs effectively, we have to persuade students on a regular basis without them being able to pinpoint our efforts.

In order to teach persuasion as a skill, there must be a lot of frontloading and ongoing practice. Time spent on persuasion is well worth it once the skill is learned and effectively utilized.

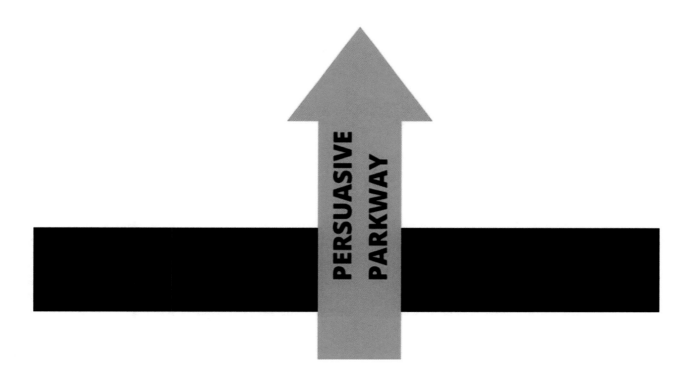

READY, SET, GO!

Persuasive Parkway Activities

+ Fight for a Cause (Heart Matters)

+ Argue Diplomatically (Philosophical Chairs)

+ Play "Name That Appeal" (An Ode to Aristotle and Advertising)

+ Workshop Those Outlines (Persuasive Bootcamp)

+ Make Moves (Speed Debating)

+ Pitch Persuasively (Sharks in the Classroom)

+ Address America (Letter and PSA)

PLANNING

THE ♥ OF
PERSUASION

ELA

Fight For A Cause
Getting to the Heart of the Matter

So many layers have to be peeled in persuasion. Scaffolding is important for students to really understand and later use these elements effectively.

Here is one of my favorite activities to open a unit on persuasion. I don't reveal the end result to students as much as I take them through a crafty soul-searching session, building on one idea after the other. Most students want to rely on something outside of themselves, and I encourage them to trust the process as it unfolds.

Being a visual person, I want to present them with certain initial experiences that are symbolic to persuasion.

At the door, I pass out pink or red sheets that will soon represent their passion.

Here, you will find:

- Teacher pink sheet **sample** that displays me getting down to the matters of my heart (it will soon be a protest sign)
- The **steps** I walk students through with my teacher model
- A **frame** with built-in questions and directions. I provide this before students start writing.

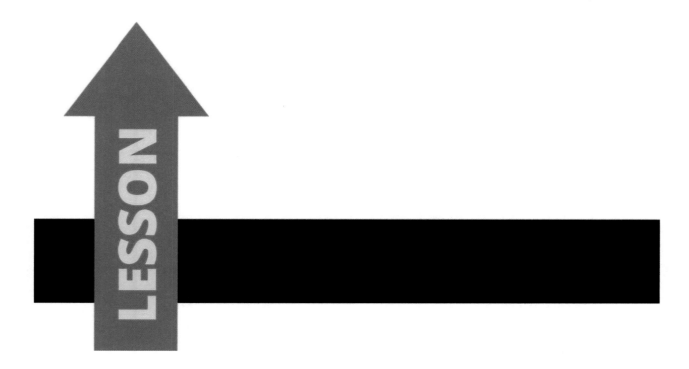

Heart Matters

The heart does not have to be perfectly drawn, nor does the writing have to be perfect. The choices just have to be true, reflective, and organic responses to the questions posed. This prewrite can later be used to expand into a more polished draft.

Step one
What are you fighting for? What do you stand for?
Put the cause in the middle of the sheet.
Write it big.
Write it proudly.

Step two
Get to the heart of the matter. Flip to the back and draw a heart in the center of the page. Inside the heart, put your "Why". Why is this important to you?
(25 points)

Step three
Find inspiration
(quote /author/ source/ correct format/ correct quality = 25 points each)
Who has already fought this fight and has advice for you?

Find 3 people who are speaking about the issue already.
Give them credit and where the information was published.
(quote/author/site/correct format/correct quality = 25 points each)

Example: On the opening of his new film studio which Perry owns outright...

"I clearly believe that I'm ignored in Hollywood...My audience and the stories that I tell are African-American stories specific to a certain audience, specific to a certain group of people that I know, that I grew up, and we speak a language...Hollywood doesn't necessarily speak the language. A lot of critics don't speak that language....I know what I do is important...I know what that does for the people where I come from and the people that I'm writing for. So, yeah, I get that" (Tyler Perry).

Site
https://www.foxnews.com/entertainment/tyler-perry-tv-film-studio-atlanta-ignored-hollywood

Step four
Find a support group. Hold up your sign in order to express what you are fighting for. Form a family of commonalities and link and stand with them. Let someone speak as to why or how you all were able to determine this group.

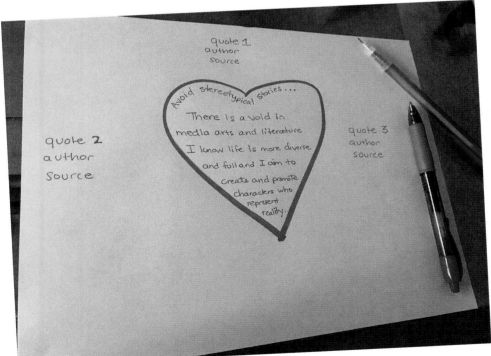

Teacher Model "FIGHT FOR THE CAUSE" PAPER with CREDIBLE SOURCES

Using the outline format below, type your answers in fully elaborated sentences in their prospective paragraphs on your own document.

Hook: **Thesis:** What are you fighting for and why is the cause so important? *(Use a form of pathos and logos for this section)*	I love music, but the last time I listened to the radio, I couldn't help but cringe. I couldn't hear "my" story. I heard great beats but when forced to listen to words, I was offended. Can you imagine living in a world where your image is obsolete? Reading book after book, you are not seeing yourself in the characters so many gush over. Even with watching tons of TV, you are not able to see your reflection. The idea of more stereotypes taking center stage than your truth, is really not as far-fetched as it seems. Studies have proven that if a person is not able to see their truth outside of themselves, they may never amount to their full potential, but rather succumb to a mockery of it. There is a void in media, arts, and literature that needs to be filled. To help fill that void, we each have a part to play: My part, as an Indie-storyteller is creating content that showcases diverse women of color from the south who are overcoming obstacles.
Support 1 Idea 1: Who is Inspiration 1? What are they known for? Why are they credible in your research? Idea 2: What route do they express or suggest should be taken to accomplish some aspect of your cause/goal? Idea 3: How did they use appeals? How effective were these appeals?	Filmmaker, Ava Duvernay is most known for her_____. In an *Essence* interview, she expresses "_____" and "_____". With a ____ tone, she uses logos to break down the concrete way to finance a project. With her ___ year old career, she effectively_____ while _____ others to go after their passions.
Support 2 Who is Inspiration 2? **(Same guiding questions as Support 1)**	Media mogul, Oprah Winfrey is a household name and a poster child for success. There is only one Oprah, but she gives great advice to women who are hoping to _____ with "_____." One can glean from her latest success that _____. *Forbes* notes that she "_____". With a ___ tone, this statement proves that through _____ and _____ one can ____.
Support 3 Who is Inspiration 3? **(Same guiding questions as Support 1)**	Indie artist, turned superstar, Chance the Rapper, has climbed the charts in recent years with his _____ music. The _____ native attributes his success to _____ as he shares "_____" (Medium.com). He is able to capture a generation of creatives and inspire them because _____. By appealing to ____, one can learn that _____in order to___.
Conclusion: Taking advice from your chosen muses, how are you going about fighting for this cause? What strategy can you put together based on the knowledge you have acquired above? *(Build ethos)*	As a teacher, writer, and creative I know stories can make or break us. With more narratives emerging and options outside of the traditional realm, I know through _____ , ____, and _____, I can continue to use Indie Storytelling as a powerful tool for helping to represent more diverse truths in our society.

Argue Diplomatically with Philosophical Chairs

Mimicking a debate structure, philosophical chairs is a great topic-based framework and practice that works well as a precursor to argumentative writing and Socratic seminars, a more text-based framework. From The San Diego County Office of Education, I've adapted philosophical chairs into an introduction to making **concessions** (agreeing to some aspect of the argument that is valid) and **refutations** (proving your argument is more credible/valid than the counter-arguments) for my 10 - 11th graders. Philosophical chairs can be group-centered with time factored in for researching topics and building arguments.

Here, you'll find:
- **Participation Directions** (verbally walking them through the process)
- **Questions** and **controversial quotes** (ranging from light to heavy topics)
- **Reflective questions** to use as a diagnostic tool, that segues into a deeper look at elements of persuasion.

Classroom Designated Areas	Content Preparation
Left side - **Agree** Right side - **Disagree** Middle section should be abandoned. No one is allowed to be on the fence.	- A screen that projects Google slides or Microsoft Powerpoint presentation. Poster board anchor charts can work as an option if you don't have technology in your class. - Create a set of questions or comments that will ignite a debate ranging in tone.
Skills - A verbal and physical representation of making **concessions** (acknowledgment of opponent's side) and **refutations** (emphasis of why your side is more valid)	**Benefits** Students learn to: - think on their feet, literally - listen carefully - debate in a civil manner.

Argue Diplomatically with Philosophical Chairs
Teachers will need to maintain order and offer constructive feedback.

Teacher Directions

1. Before the discussion begins, students are given a moment to read each statement or question that is presented.
2. Students are given another minute (or several seconds) to think about where they stand on the issue.
3. If they agree, they should move to the left side of the room. Disagree? Move to the right side. No one should stand in the middle. But *if* someone changes their mind along the way, they are free to switch sides, quietly.

Once everyone is in place, the debate over the issue begins.

4. The side with the majority starts the conversation/debate. One person has the floor to voice their stance (without interruption).
5. One person from the opposing side makes a concession to some aspect of the starting argument before making their own point. THEN, their argument is made (without interruption).
6. Returning to the starting team, step #2 takes place with a different student speaking.

- The process is repeated multiple times as needed and as time allows to continue the debate.

Side conversations are not allowed. Students are practicing both listening and speaking skills.

You may choose to teach CONCESSIONS & REFUTATIONS before, during, or after the activity. I have heard from teachers who later inherited my students that these were strengths in their writing, and I equate that strength to working this activity into the persuasive unit, using it not only as a real life diplomacy tactic, but practice with working counter arguments into their natural back-and-forth dialogue. This may take a moment for many students to get used to, but thinking on their feet during in-class debates seems to have a lasting effect in their writing.

Philosophical Chairs Questions

Forming Concessions and Refutations

Stand in the agree or disagree section. No one can stand in the middle. In other words, don't straddle the fence. You must pick a side. Make a concession before you debate and argue your case.

1. We have it harder than our parents.
2. Everyone would be a lot better off without social media.
3. Hard work beats talent any day.
4. Computer crimes should receive harsher penalties and punishments.
5. If college is not in your future, you have no future.
6. Discussions about religion should be allowed in school.
7. Schools should have courses on race relations.
8. Bullies are really bullied people.
9. More men need to be househusbands.
10. Some books should be banned.
11. A sense of humor can carry you further than a sense of entitlement.
12. Judging a book by its cover comes with negative consequences.
13. Traditional clubs and organizations are not important to the new generation of students.
14. War has its place and is inevitable.
15. In a world of noise, the most important voice is _____.
16. People can let their emotions blind them.
17. Priorities should determine success, not _____.
18. _____
19. _____
20. _____

Philosophical Chairs
Closing Activity/Reflection Questions

- What appeal did you rely on the most to express yourself? Why?
- What makes someone an effective communicator?
- What is the difference between argument and persuasion?
- What allows a persuasive paper to be an effective argument?
- What are 5 persuasive elements that help structure your writing?
- What did you do well and what will you adjust for next time?
- What are other thoughts or comments?

Play "Name That Appeal" with Ads
(An Ode to Aristotle and Advertising)

My favorite way to get students acclimated to analyzing, as well as producing persuasive content, is through ads.

Ads, often bright and bold visuals, elicit great insight discussion and remain ingrained in our hearts and minds, depending on what appeal was dominant.

So, I provide students with a framework and notes on how to categorize the three appeals: **ethos, pathos, and logos.** This allows us to speak about ads, using common criteria. We can then evaluate each ad's dominant appeal more thoroughly.

Here, you'll find:

- A **graphic organizer** for students to record notes regarding what makes each **appeal unique.**

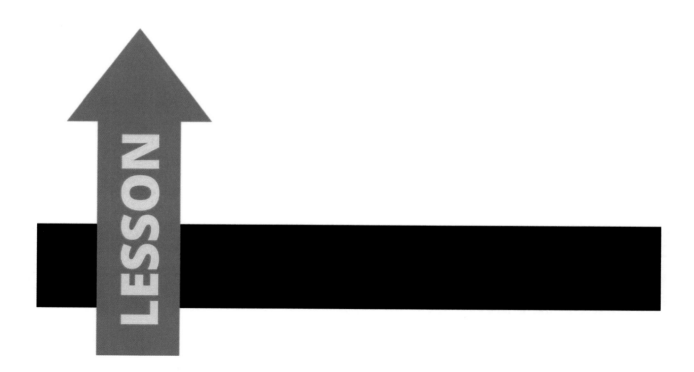

An Ode to Aristotle

Thousands of years ago, Greek Philosopher, Aristotle identified the three critical elements. Compile notes on ethos, pathos, and logos in order to successfully identify them in content as well as effectively use them in your own content.

Ethos	Pathos	Logos
Definition	Definition	Definition
Characteristics	Characteristics	Characteristics
Real world example 1	Real world example 1	Real world example 1
Real world example 2	Real world example 2	Real world example 2

Play "Name That Appeal"
(An Ode to Advertising)

Before embarking on persuasive writing, let's play a game of "Name that Appeal"

After students have taken extensive notes on each appeal, it's time to play a game to test their ability to **identify appeals** and **examine those ideas for meaning**. Controversial, thought-provoking, and interesting advertisements from various brands come in handy. I have done this with my AP Language and on-level 10th and 11th grade students.

Preparation	How to display ads:
- Pre-select about 20 advertisements that have a dominant appeal - Create class sets - 3 sets of color-coded index cards that represent each appeal	1. Projected slides 2. Hard copies posted around the room 3. Stations with hard copies 4. Online student access
Homework Students bring in their own thought-provoking ad to be examined and analyzed independently or in pairs.	**Tip:** Walk students through projected slides as a class first to create a scaffold, then let them break into small groups to evaluate ads more independently.

Here, you will find:
- **Student directions**
- A **graphic organizer** for determining appeals and messages of ads
- A **composition box** for making colorful sandwiches to expand ideas in analytical paragraphs

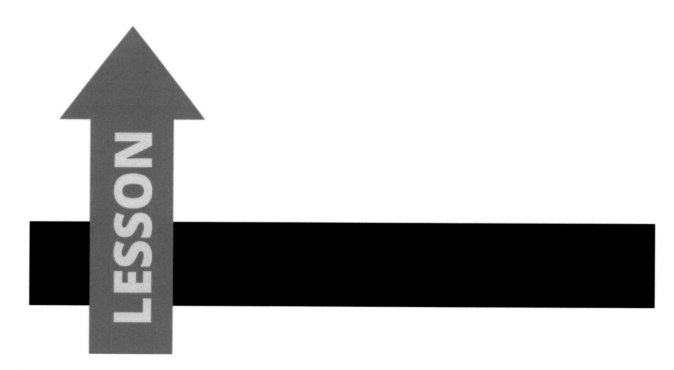

Play "Name that Appeal" Student Directions

Step one: Determine claim. THEN "Name that Appeal".

You should have three color-coded index cards or sheets on your desk. If online, answers are coded on *Kahoot* (a game-based learning platform).

Red = ethos
Blue = pathos
Yellow = logos

You will be presented with an advertisement. You will have one minute to determine what claim is being made or implied. Then, NAME THAT APPEAL by holding up the appropriate color card when time is up.

Valid Question: What if there is more than one appeal?
Valid Answer: There may be more than one appeal, but choose the most apparent or most dominant.

The sea of cards reveal your thoughts quickly. We will have a brief discussion on the dominant appeal. The students who guessed the more dominant appeal can share their reasoning.

Step two: You have some explaining to do...

For each ad, discuss what you see and what messages are being presented in the advertisement. Identify key items and add meaning to the concrete details by explaining the messages presented.

1. What do you see? (Point out key concrete objects that are not debatable, but factual.)

2. What does it mean? (What are two main messages that stem from what you see? A variety of valid viewpoints are welcome.)

Play "Name that Appeal" Student Directions

Step three: Chart Your Ideas
How does the advertiser effectively employ logos, pathos, or ethos to appeal to an audience? Determine two messages.

Teacher Model:

Ad # and brief description	Name the Dominant Appeal	Message 1	Message 2
"Declare Yourself" featuring sassy singer	Ethos	Christina Aguilera is known for her singing voice and bold attitude, so using her as a spokesperson speaks volumes.	The ad is urging the audience to speak up because one's voice is important and to silence your own ideas would be a crying shame.

Step Four: Use Your Charted Ideas to Make Colorful Sandwiches

Prompt: In an analytical paragraph, thoroughly explain how the advertiser effectively employs logos, pathos, or ethos to appeal to an audience. Determine the intended tone, message, and audience.

Colorful Sandwich ingredients
Idea 1: Answer and include ad's **TAGS** (Title, Advertiser, Genre, and Subject)
Idea 2: Provide evidence. **Embed 3 snippets** of textual evidence. (A mixture of text and paraphrases are appropriate for an ad).
Idea 3: Add your **insight** regarding the ad's intent.

Teacher Model:
With an ironically brilliant tone, the "Declare Yourself" ad, featuring sassy singer, Christina Aguilera, relies heavily on irony and ethos to ignite a call to action. The ad presents the artist in dramatic hair and make-up. Yet, her bold red lip is stitched shut by a black rope. This bound and gagged imagery, along with words in all caps and a sound wave-like font, reading "ONLY YOU CAN SILENCE YOURSELF" promotes how silence is far from golden. She is looking away, in a distance, with tears rolling down her face. With red, white, and blue color schemes, this is not a patriotic message, but instead a cautionary tale. To silence your own ideas would be a crying shame. The ad successfully urges the pop-cultured audience to speak up because one's voice is important. The former "The Voice" judge is known for her singing, voice, and bold attitude. Using her as a spokesperson speaks volumes.

Name & Explain That Appeal: Chart Your Ideas

How does the advertiser employ logos, pathos, or ethos to appeal to an audience?

Ad # and brief description	Name the Dominant Appeal	Message 1	Message 2

Name and Explain That Appeal: Make a Colorful Sandwich

Prompt: In an analytical paragraph, thoroughly explain how the advertiser effectively employs logos, pathos, or ethos to appeal to an audience. Determine the intended tone, message, and audience.

Make a colorful sandwich. Include textual evidence and your insight.

Idea 1

Idea 2

Idea 3

Workshop: Persuasive Essay Outlines

Before I use standardized test samples with my students, I use past and present revolutionary speeches. I may scramble up the speech and have my students put it back together, pinpoint the 5 elements of persuasion, or identify strong use of logos, pathos, or ethos. I think there is a lot of value in dissecting the works that have changed the world.

Working so closely with texts like this also:
1. Showcases how persuasion is used in the real world, and
2. Shows formats that are not as formulaic.

Expectations and criteria vary from state to state, but no one can deny good writing. You know what it is when you see it.

When I am working with standardized test samples, I have students guess the score and dissect the piece in similar ways we have done model texts. So here you will find an idea of how to assess students' level of understanding regarding writing skills commonly assessed on high-stakes tests.

Here, you will find:

- A **writing questionnaire** you can use as a diagnostic and later a quiz
- **Writing outline** for mapping out a timed essay
- An **essay composition sheet**
- My **writing boot camp steps** to help students evaluate their writing and see how to enhance rough draft

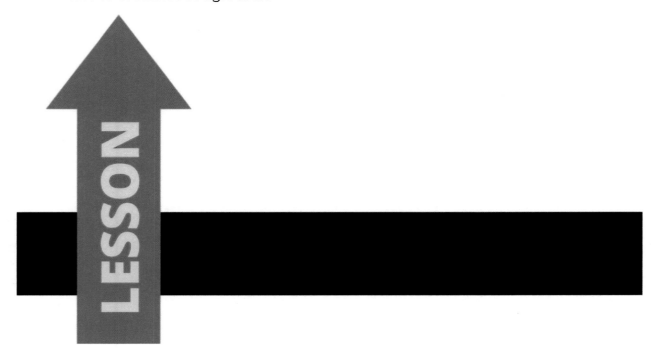

Writing Talk

1. What is the difference between an outline and an essay?

2. How much time does it take to draft both? Why?

3. In regards to position, purpose, and elements, what are the differences between a persuasive and expository piece?

4. When do you take your standardized test? (Note this year's date.)

5. For the essay portion, is there a line or page limit for your essay? If so, what is the limit? How many lines? How many pages?

Workshop: Persuasive Essay Outlines

20-Minute Challenge:

You will be assigned a random topic. Using past notes and samples, as a form of prewriting, create effective statements (not paragraphs) that present ideas you'll later expand and elaborate in an actual persuasive essay. Be persuasive! Structure your potential essay!

Persuasive Elements	In this box, copy the prompt, topic, or claim
Hook (i.e. quote, joke, shocker. Avoid questions...)	_____ _____ _____
Thesis Thesis Pieces 1. State your one-sided argument/ claim 2. And a bit of reasoning)	_____ _____ _____
Support 1 + Support 2 **What helps prove your claim?** - Research-based statistics & scientific data - Current or historical events - Anecdotal (short scenarios experiences)	_____ _____ _____ _____ _____
Concession + Refutation (Briefly nod to your opponent on one of their points, but ultimately, let them know where you stand)	_____ _____ _____
Call to Action (You can be bossy here)	_____ _____

Writing Workshop: Persuasive Essay 30-Minute Limit

_____

_____

_____

_____

_____

_____

_____

_____

_____

_____

_____

_____

_____

_____

_____

_____

_____

_____

_____

_____

_____

_____

_____

_____

_____

Workshop: Writing BOOTCAMP

Each scaffolded section is timed. Factoring in essay samples and rubric expectations, return to a persuasive essay rough draft in order to take it through a series of steps that will help you evaluate your work and improve your writing.

Points earned	Ordered steps and student checklist
_____ _____ _____ _____ _____ _____ _____	**_____Return to the prompt.** **In red pen, dissect it by marking the text.** **Brainstorm. Remember the purpose and position one would take when preparing a persuasive paper.** **_____Return to the essay to color code it.** - **Make a Colorful Sandwich key at the top of your paper.** - **Remind yourself what each idea means.** - **With highlighters that coincide with each of the three ideas, highlight each sentence of the essay with the appropriate color. Choose thoughtfully.** **_____ Label 5 elements in red pen** - **Label/initial, at the start of the idea, what there is evidence of: (H, T, S1, S2, C+R CTA).** - **You will lose points if you randomly mark elements. You will earn points for honestly marking what is actually there.** **_____Circle 10 weak words** **What is weighing down your paper?** **_____Upgrade those 10 weak words.** **Write the replacement above in red.** **Use a thesaurus to enhance your paper with appropriate words.** **_____Guess what score you earned, based on the rubric provided.** **Give 4 reasons why.** **On the back of your paper, write "Guessed Score". Beside it, write the score you predict. Use 4 pieces of evidence from the rubric to support the score you are guessing.** **_____Reflect on areas (Refer to the Reflection section for prompt.)**
Total points earned _____	**Teacher notes/comments:**

Make Moves with Speed Debating

I love discount stores and bargains. I was happy to find "Agree or Disagree" cards in the clearance section of *Home Goods*. They covered a number of debatable topics. I was excited to use them in class.

There are many forms of debate on the high school and collegiate level. There are also plenty of debatable issues that can be discussed in the classroom to help students sharpen many skills. Here is how I use them in my class:

Like in spontaneous argumentation, two debaters are given a random topic. In this case, during short rotations, students cover a lot of ground, moving from one topic to another, expressing their argument over various issues.	**Things to Note:** - Students' prior knowledge ranges and there should not be much prep time. - Similar to debate, students may have to present from a side they would normally not.
Before and After **Before -** Students can take what is done with Philosophical Chairs to a new level. They can push themselves to use all 5 elements covered in class as a framework for their conversation. **After -** Students can research some of the issues they were not as familiar with to gain insight on the topic.	**Benefits** - Verbal practice helps develop style - Helps decrease speaker anxiety - Insight gained from peers - Greater familiarity with the elements of persuasion

Here, you will find:
- A couple of my **favorite debate topics** (I have made **mini cards** for your table)
- A **graphic organizer** for students to track their thoughts and rate their peers

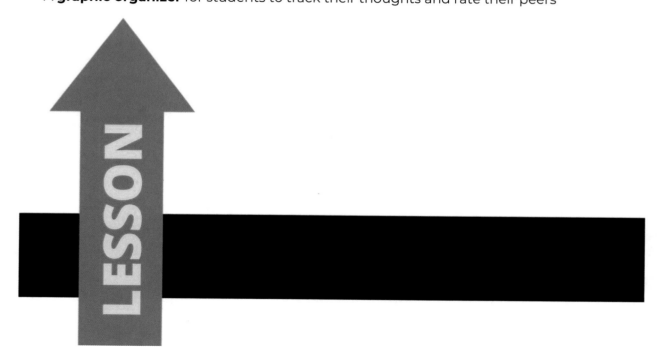

16 Speed Debating Topics

Diets are healthy. Diets are harmful.	The prison system is a form of punishment. The prison system is a form of profit.	Gentrification helps the neighborhood. Gentrification harms the neighborhood.	Who's to blame for global warming? Can anything be done about reversing it?
Video games are dangerous. Video games are harmless.	There is hope for Generation Z. Generation Z is doomed.	Vaccinations need to be optional. Vaccinations need to be mandatory.	Homework is a waste of time. Homework is worth the time.
What is your take on managing the types of gender bathrooms?	Social Media hinders today's youth. Social Media benefits today's youth.	Who should pay for health insurance?	Plastic surgery is not acceptable. Plastic surgery is acceptable.
What's your take on gun control?	Desegregation: Success or failure?	For or against: self-driving cars	What number one advice would you give parents?

Make Moves with Speed Debating

Element	classmate 1 Topic	classmate 2 Topic	classmate 3 Topic	classmate 4 Topic	classmate 5 Topic
Hook (rate from 1-5)					
Thesis (rate from 1-5)					
Support (rate from 1-5 and list their poster child or current event)					
Concession & Refutation (rate from 1-5)					
Call to action (rate from 1-5)					

My Praise Report goes to _____

Give 3 reasons why they deserve it...

Reason 1.

Reason 2.

Reason 3.

This Praise Report was given by (Write Your Name)

_____

Pitch Persuasively with SHARKS in the Classroom

I am always looking for ways to make real-world connections with my students. A couple of years back, after a conversation with my mom, a retired business teacher, I had an idea for an upcoming unit. For years, in her Accounting and Global Business classes, she used the popular TV show, *Shark Tank*, as an engagement tool and model for their projects. Being a fan of the show, I knew that effective pitching skills are needed AND are transferable. I was excited and wanted to find a way to align the concept of pitching products with the ELA standards. I knew my students needed to be prepared to pitch ideas in the future and for some, the near future. I created a week-long project for my juniors for their persuasive unit. As team lead that year, I shared it with the other junior teachers. The results were awesome, and it has been an annual tradition, not only in our department, but in two other departments on campus ever since.

Here, you'll find:
- The **full pitch lesson** inspired by *Shark Tank,* which includes **pre-pitch activities, prewriting outlines, peer score sheet, teacher grading guidelines for live pitch and post pitch questions.**

Things to think about - Who will be your **ELA Sharks?** I have invited local business pros for two years. I have also invited school officials. Some other teachers utilized students. Find what works best for your group.

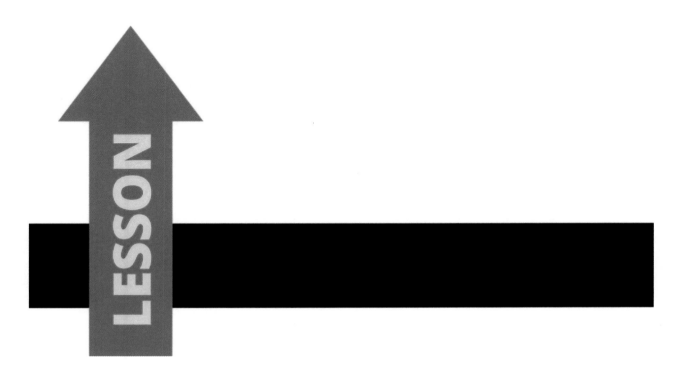

The Script

Teacher / Host: Welcome to the Lit for Life Studios! We are here to celebrate the art of persuasion! Teams are here to pitch their ideas: They are here to Heal The World. Pitches consist of 5 persuasive elements. Judges are here to pose questions after your pitch and possibly give you a deal! (Smile for the camera!)

While pitches are taking place, audience members will score each group. The group with the highest total points will be circled on your page before turning it in for your daily grade. You will get your final grade from me.

So who will be The Crowd favorite?

Let me cover a couple of house rules:

1. Earn points; don't lose them by having side conversations.
2. Let's give each group the attention they deserve. They are here to HEAL THE WORLD!

Who will get a deal from The Sharks? STAY TUNED...

Pitch Persuasively With SHARKS in the Classroom

OBJECTIVE

Students, in small groups of 5, are to present a 5-minute persuasive pitch for their fictional or nonfictional product that addresses a real-world issue or need, literally or figuratively. Each student, having a distinct role in conception and presentation, will present their team product in front of a panel of expert judges and a live studio audience (classmates). After their pitch, they should be prepared and able to answer 3 questions from a pool of questions from the potential sponsors regarding how effective this product is or will be, while being judged on how persuasive they are.

While pitches are presented, classmates are responsible for completing a checklist rating below for a daily grade. 5 points will be added to the crowd favorite on their overall major grade (those who score higher total points in the class get that bonus).

Suggested Roles:
- Time Keeper - ensures deadlines are met
- Leader - ensures everyone participates
- Scribe - writes everything down
- Runner - gathers supplies, communicates with teacher
- Encourager - ensures everyone is on task with a positive morale

Pre-Pitch:
- Form a group
- Swap contact information
- Determine roles
- Create a shared Google doc/presentation to create pitch
- Do research to determine a real-world problem
- Answer the following 6 questions to ensure your problem is focused
    - Who?
    - What?
    - When?
    - Where?
    - Why?
    - How?
- Problem approved by teacher _____
- Go back to group and develop a product that solves the problem
- Use **Post-Pitch Questions** to focus your product
- Product approved by teacher _____
- Begin working on pitch
- Fill in **Persuasive Outline**
- Persuasive Outline approved by teacher _____
- Create presentation based on Persuasive Outline

Peer Scoring Rubric

Your Name_____

Class Period___ Observed Group #___ Product Name_____

Hook circle one: ineffective 1 2 3 4 5 effective
Thesis circle one: ineffective 1 2 3 4 5 effective
Support 1 and 2 circle one: ineffective 1 2 3 4 5 effective
Concession and Refutation circle one: ineffective 1 2 3 4 5 effective
Call to action circle one: ineffective 1 2 3 4 5 effective

Total points (add all categories above) _____

Your Name_____

Class Period___ Observed Group #___ Product Name_____

Hook circle one: ineffective 1 2 3 4 5 effective
Thesis circle one: ineffective 1 2 3 4 5 effective
Support 1 and 2 circle one: ineffective 1 2 3 4 5 effective
Concession and Refutation circle one: ineffective 1 2 3 4 5 effective
Call to action circle one: ineffective 1 2 3 4 5 effective

Total points (add all categories above) _____

Your Name_____

Class Period___ Observed Group #___ Product Name_____

Hook circle one: ineffective 1 2 3 4 5 effective
Thesis circle one: ineffective 1 2 3 4 5 effective
Support 1 and 2 circle one: ineffective 1 2 3 4 5 effective
Concession and Refutation circle one: ineffective 1 2 3 4 5 effective
Call to action circle one: ineffective 1 2 3 4 5 effective

Total points (add all categories above) _____

Persuasive Pitch Outline

Together, the team will complete this outline. A hard copy/printed copy will need to be handed in when you walk in for the pitch. The persuasive pitch should present a product that solves the problem, is approved by the teacher, and contains 5 persuasive essay elements below, in that order. This is checked ahead of time for a daily grade and in time for you to make changes for improvement before presenting to the panel of judges.

Piece of the pitch	Writing Pointers	brainstorm/outline of possible statements
Hook	Use any of the **appeals** to **engage** your audience from the start. Maybe you need to be charming with a purpose or a rebel with a cause or informing to the masses. Right away, showcase the **problem** in the world.	
Thesis	Your major claim (state your product's name) should be a **solution** to the problem. Share your plan and what you are here to do and then insert what you need from your intended audience. (i.e. Money?)	
Support 1 and 2	1 and 2: Explain the purpose of the product/demonstrate how it works. Share logos: Provide statistics/ research to help support your claim.	
Concession and Refutation	Acknowledge how your opposer/hater has a point. State the possible point, but explain how your points are more credible, valid, etc.	
Call-to-action	Reiterate what you want for this product to come to life with a command, request, offer, etc.	

After you are graded on the scale of 1 - 5 (3 is standard), you can disseminate the information strategically for a presentation (computer presentation, posters, brochures, etc).

The Pitch Grading Sheet

Share material for the judges in a strategic way that showcases a persuasive outline.

Group # ___ and members_____
Product_____
Presentation Scoring (each section is worth 20 points)

_____**Clear and compelling presentation** - The thesis is clear and every member presents, in a balanced way, something important. The presentation flows all the way to the end.

_____**Original idea** - The product is thoughtful and unique (not on every shelf already). You have done your research and know what else is already out there and why your product is better.

_____**Organized and natural structured argument -** effectiveness of original writing presented in visuals

_____**Authenticity** - The product and the need for the product feel real.

_____**Source Page -** Links/titles are sufficient.

_____**TOTAL POINTS**

POST PITCH (our SHARKS)
The judges (economics / health / social sciences) may ask you any of these questions at the end. So make sure to prepare an answer.

1. How many other things are like this out on the market?
2. Will you accept an offer of____ instead?
3. Who are your customers?
4. What need does your invention address?
5. What's the product category?
6. Why will consumers/customers/clients buy your product/service?
7. What is the current primary alternative to your product?
8. What's the primary differentiation?

Address America with a Letter

I think personification is underrated in high school classrooms. This literary device can open up a world of interesting writing.

After teaching through a couple of hurricane seasons, in some way, shape, or form, we have returned to class impacted. I wanted to find writing exercises that could help students cope with the reality that their homes were destroyed or lives were turned upside down. I would find ways to factor in time to let many vent, getting those emotions out through writing directly to Hurricane Ike, Rita, Harvey so they could give the storm a piece of their mind.

I have learned that these types of writings have been more than just an assignment. One student even told me activities like this helped her come out of depression.

So when teaching AP students, students who are, on a daily basis, immersed in current events and topics where they can exercise their voice, I thought it would be great to allow them to address the very country they call home.

Here, you'll find:

- A **personified prompt** for **addressing America**
- **PSA Creation** Group Challenge

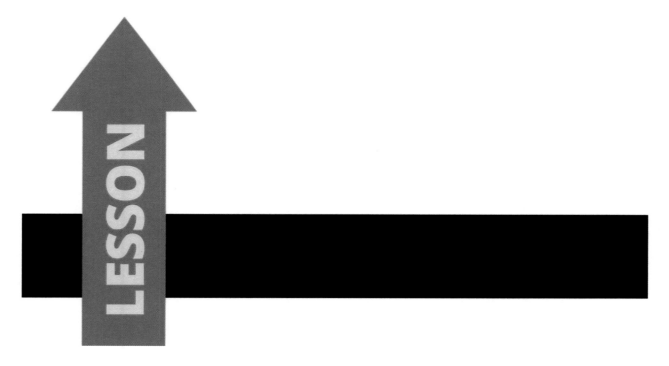

Dear America Writing Assignment

Create a letter to America. As you talk to dear America, use personification to your advantage. Remember the purpose of persuasion and the elements that allow it to be distinctive. Use your brainstorming to communicate your ideas in the most effective way. The final letter needs to be at least one page.

Make sure to factor in the questions below in a meaningful way.

PRE WRITING

I.   How are you going to get America's attention?

II.   What is your biggest claim?

Why is this your point of view/perspective on the subject?

III.   How will you support your position?

Do you have a praise report for her? Or do you have concerns?

What advice or aphorisms would you share?

IV.   What are others' points of view on her?

V.   What would be your call-to-action: your ultimate plea?

- Make sure to sign and date your letter.

Address America with a PSA

A public service announcement (PSA), or public service ad, is a message in the public interest disseminated without charge, with the objective of raising awareness and changing public attitudes and behavior towards a social issue (Wikipedia, the Free Encyclopedia).

You and your classmates will need to join forces to determine how you all can create one effective **PSA.** Focusing on strong examples, in your group, **include the following:**

1. Hook
2. Thesis
3. Support 1 + 2
4. Concession + Refutation
5. Call To Action

_____**All members should be involved** in some way:
(writing/ acting/ camera/ editing/ uploading/ timekeeper/ scene selector)

_____**The Script Must be Approved in Advance**
The handwritten hardcopy or printed typed copy can serve as an outline and is worth **50 points.** Look at the above elements and produce a compelling script based on this structure.

_____**The Video Must Reflect the Approved Script**
Consider appropriate video and audio elements. Make sure they are presentable. The uploaded final video is worth another **50 points.**

Consider the following that are worth 10 points each:
- Clear cause
- Originality
- Authenticity
- Wise use of time
- Uploaded on time

_____The **1-minute video** should be correctly uploaded by the deadline to earn the rest of your team's points. We will watch all of them!

REFLECTION AVENUE

DEAR TEACHER,

At the time of writing this book, we were in the middle of a pandemic, one that is continually changing the way we not only *teach*, but do life. We cannot help but reflect on how massive the shifts have been and on how we will forever be changed from this point forth, one way or another. The shift from in-class instruction to virtual came abruptly and lasted longer than many expected. In articles like, *4 Tips for Teachers Shifting to Teaching Online*, one way that distance learning can be made possible is through individual touch points. **INDIVIDUAL TOUCHPOINTS are game changers.** Farah writes, "While it can be tempting to focus on content in your distance learning assignments and instructional videos, what matters more is creating structures for personalized touchpoints with your students." Taking a moment to reflect and express those reflections is crucial now more than ever.

Aside from a pandemic, high school is already such an unforgettable time and experience in a person's life. Each year adds a new layer of understanding and identity. It would be a shame to not include time for pure reflection as well as academics. Similar to the opening chapter, where vision boards are the focus, here is a place where those early aspirations can be revisited through discussion and writing.

Life is a great teacher. Learning environments that encourage students to think independently, by weighing out their own thoughts in a concise and educated manner, challenge them to use knowledge as their tools in order to draw conclusions that will allow them to have success, not only in but also outside the classroom!

SELF CARE

SCRIPTURE	INSPIRATION
"For now we see in a mirror dimly, but then face to face. Now I know in part; then I shall know fully, even as I have been fully known." **1 Corinthians 13:12**	"Everyone and everything that shows up in our life is a reflection of something that is happening inside of us." **Alan Cohen**

Real life...

Ultimately, this book has been shaped by the students I have taught. Reading their writing reflections at the end of each unit and conducting individual writing conferences played a part in me growing effectively as a teacher.

Hearing from students about their own reflections, evaluations of their strengths and weaknesses, and their *aha* moments, has helped shape not only this edition, but has enlightened my teaching from year-to-year.

What is life without thoughtful reflection? I want to infuse parts of mindfulness in the classroom when it matters most. Having space (spiral notebooks, journals, writing portfolios, flash drives, online drives) and time supports our students' processing, coping, and thinking.

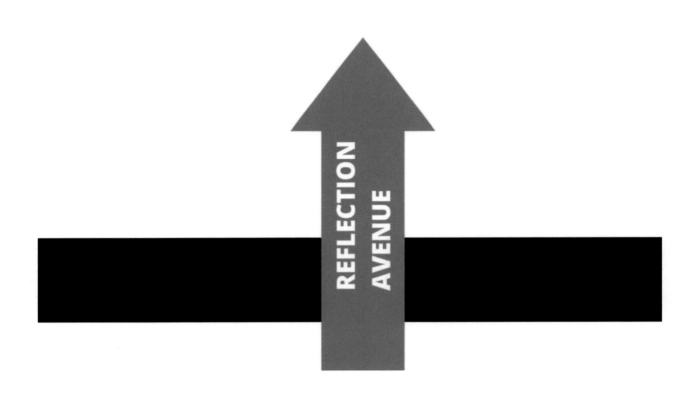

READY, SET, GO!

Reflection Avenue Activities

+ Levels to this...The World as a Snapshot

+ Workshop: Timed Writing Boot Camp

+ Build Vocabulary

+ Reflect On Your Reading

+ Read Daily For Reflection Entries

+ Write A One-Page Reflection

+ Reflect on diverse POV of the Same Topic

+ Reflect On Your Own Writing

PLANNING

... At an in-service in my current district, teachers were assigned reflection time to think about the books that shaped us and changed our lives. We then had to draw our, "My Ideal Bookshelf "- based on a book with the same title. *Here is mine.*

We later wrote a personal essay as an extension. I love ideas like these. We were encouraged to have our students do the same thing ...

WHAT'S GOING ON?

REALITY CHECK-IN

...Levels to this...

What is the current snapshot of our global, local, personal world?

Keeping abreast of current events, whether through strategies like SOAPSTONE, card games found in the clearance section named, "Real News vs. Fake News", the popular AP students' strategy *$SEEITT*, or AVID reflection starters, constant conversation about the world outside of the classroom surely helps to inform us and our students of what is important and why. Being reflective is one of the first steps to being effective in reading and writing. Reflection is prompted by a form of questioning.

Reflection also plays a part in building prior knowledge and background knowledge that proves helpful with tests that address broad topics. The classroom is also a place to define things and to acknowledge the gravity of a moment. We can challenge what is considered newsworthy.

Here, you'll find:
Next up is a composition sheet that can be used for students' timed essays. These essays will be used later for reflection purposes.

- **Common AVID Reflection Starters**
- **Timed Writing Composition** sheet for reflection
- Another **Writing Bootcamp** set of steps that can be used to revisit past work

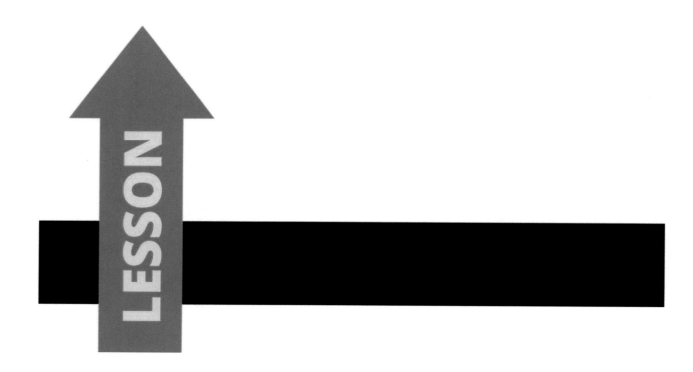

AVID Reflection Starters

-This is important because
-One way this strategy helped me
-As a reader, I feel
-As a writer, I am
-This reminds me of
-Now I understand that
-One thing I can do
-It appears/seems to me that
-I'm struggling with
-What's interesting about this is
-What I find a bit
-One challenge that I am finding
-Others may believe that
-What I'd like to know is
-I will use this when I

Workshop - Timed Writing *30-Minute Limit*

Workshop: BOOTCAMP

Return to an earlier draft of your writing in order to reflect on areas of strengths and weaknesses. Each scaffolded section is timed. Factoring in essay samples and rubric expectations, return to an earlier rough draft and take it through a series of steps that will help you evaluate your work and improve your writing.

1. Return to the prompt

In red pen, dissect it by marking the text. Brainstorm.
Remember the purpose and position one would take when preparing a _____ paper.

2. Return to the essay to color-code it

- **Make a Colorful Sandwich key at the top of your paper.**
- **Remind yourself of what each idea means.**
- **With highlighters that coincide with each of the three ideas, highlight each sentence of the essay with the appropriate color. Choose thoughtfully.**

3. Label 5 elements in red pen

- **Label/initial, at the start of the idea, what there is evidence of:**

  _____

- **You will lose points if you randomly mark elements. You will earn points for honestly marking what is actually there.**

4. Circle 10 weak words

What is weighing down your paper?

Upgrade those 10 weak words - write the replacement above in red.
Use a thesaurus to enhance your paper with appropriate words.

5. Guess what score you earned based on the rubric provided. Give 4 reasons why.
On the back of your paper, write "Guessed Score". Beside it, write the score you predict. Use 4 pieces of evidence from the rubric to support the score you are guessing.
Reflect on areas (Refer to the Reflection section for prompt.)

Build Vocabulary

I know what many people are thinking: Why would any high school student need to define advanced vocabulary words? It's funny how many leaders don't like this type of assignment carried out in class, but after reading 150 essays per assignment, I beg to differ.

So whether the advanced, academic, specialized, or targeted words for your ELA pupils are teacher-assigned or student-chosen, whether you allow dictionaries or phones to be their resources, or whether you have them utilize the words correctly in some sort of writing assignment afterwards, I believe it is necessary to make vocabulary a classroom norm.

Building vocabulary should be an ongoing, long-term activity. Robert Marzano is known for his recommendation that students maintain academic vocabulary notebooks where words are defined and even constructed, and that these logs are revisited and maintained throughout the year in order to increase long-term retention. What I have been told first hand in over 45 one-on-ones with students in various grade levels is that they crave building their vocabulary.

I always tell students when writing essays, especially standardized ones: Imagine me, or graders of hundreds of essays with the same prompt. Imagine trying not to fall asleep because it all starts to sound the same. AND THEN A PIECE COMES ALONG WITH COLORFUL LANGUAGE THAT MAKES YOU WAKE UP!

Here, you'll find:
- A **Big Ten graphic organizer** that can be placed in students' binders as a year-long template. These words can also be added to the **class word wall** before and after quizzes and games.

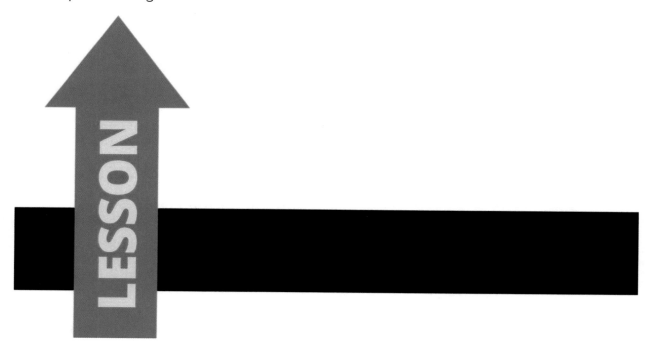

BIG TEN Vocabulary Rectangles

You are to pull 10 academically advanced or colorful words from the reading or dictionary. Define, dissect, and describe them in order to expand your vocabulary. (You cannot use advanced words you already know.) Copy the format below and fill in each rectangle with the appropriate information. Be sure to number all ten vocabulary boxes. These words will be used again in a separate assessment.

Vocabulary Word: Synonym:	Part(s) of Speech:	Definition:
Visual Representation:		

Don't worry if you are not Picasso - do your best visual representation!

Reflect On Your Reading

We never forget the work of others that move us.

We can give credit where it is due and examine what makes it special, what makes good writing good.

This can motivate and empower us as writers.

As we dealt with the unexpected at the end of the spring 2020 semester (a pandemic that changed not only the course of how we would teach our students, but the world at-large) we knew that we needed something that would allow students to become leaders in their own learning.

The district I worked in wanted us to primarily check on the students' well-being and continue to focus on infusing daily reading and writing into this new schedule. Here is what I gave my students who were no longer in front of me, but off in the distance on a regular basis. These activities work well with virtual learning as well as in the traditional classroom.

Here, you'll find:
- Student instructions for **daily reflection journal entries**
- Student directions for the **one-page reflection writing assignment** that follows the reflection journals
- **Teacher model** provided upon assigning these writing reflections as a reference for the **one-page reflection writing assignment**

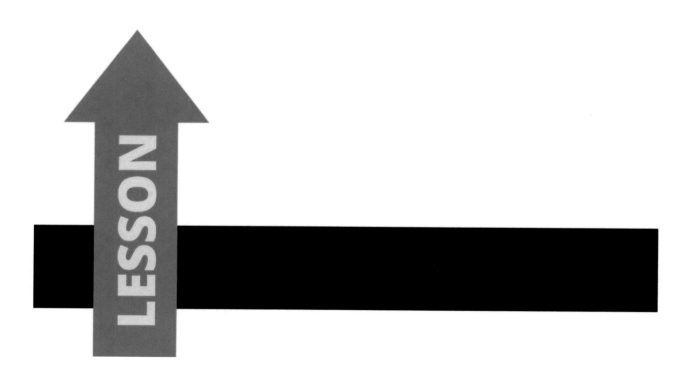

Read Daily for Reflection

For 30 minutes of independent reading time, students should be actively engaging with a variety of artistic content daily.

Each day, select from the menu below. Select one option per day and reflect on your reading and share your text impression. (You won't be able to repeat these in one week. They can only be used once in a week). Make sure to also integrate advanced vocabulary you have been learning this year.

>   **Option 1** Article that was written this month
>   **Option 2** Movie script, play, or monologue
>   **Option 3** Song lyrics
>   **Option 4** Poem
>   **Option 5** Speech transcript
>   **Option 6** Editorial
>   **Option 7** Novel
>   **Option 8** Nonfiction book

For journal entries, include your heading:
Your name and class period at the top of your page.

Follow the daily tasks below.

Daily Notebook Response Format:

1. Option number
2. Title of Piece
3. Author
4. Your reflection (a paragraph)

You should be turning in 5 entries in the form of meaningful paragraphs by the end of the week.

Write a One-Page Reflection

Students should be actively engaging with a variety of artistic content that can serve as inspiration, research, or context for their reflection process. Students should submit a one-page reflection using one of the options below. They should discuss what they've read and their insight. Each one-page reflection should be 500 words minimum. Refer to the teacher model.

READING OPTIONS: *Take one of the earlier readings and expand on that idea.*

Independent Reading Time and Writing Time

Each day, work on perfecting each paragraph of your reflection.
This should be your own original work, thoughts, and analysis. I want to read what you think.

DON'T forget to include:
- heading (look at the teacher model)
- *one-sentence summary* **(10 points)**

In any order, each paragraph should touch on the following:
- What is your favorite aspect of the writing? **(20 points)**
- Least favorite aspect of the piece? **(20 points)**
- Author's intent? **(20 points)**
- Textual evidence to explain one literary element? **(10 points)**
- Effect on the audience? **(20 points)**

Look at my teacher model for the format. Sample on next page.

DEADLINE _____
1. Add a new page/ document and start typing or upload a neatly-written page.
2. Turn your page in on Google Classrooms or _____. CLICK TURN IN or SUBMIT.

ANALYST: Micole Williams
OPTION 2: Script
TITLE: *Little Women*
AUTHOR: Greta Gerwig
GENRE: HISTORICAL Drama/Period Piece
CIRCA: Civil War LOCALE: America

One-page Reflection
TEACHER MODEL

One Sentence Summary
In this coming-of-age tale, Jo March, the writer of the March sisters, through a series of trials and celebrations, finds her voice.

My Favorite Part
This story moves like poetry. The project is an exciting rendition of an endearing classic that touches the hearts of many who not only have a dream, but have a plan for it to become reality. It is a personal view of the makings of a writer in a time when women are hushed, more than today. The script seamlessly weaves together flashbacks that make the present scenes more meaningful. With all their flaws, the artistic women are authentically intriguing. With a fresh approach, this may be the best of all the *Little Women* versions to date.

Author's Intent - Explain at least one literary element and add textual evidence to support your claim.
Fire **is a major motif,** literally and figuratively, in the script. For those of us who grew up reading this story, this remake is the one that makes you feel like someone is able to capture the fire that the book possesses but in a new and interesting way! These characters **burn** through the pages, just like the book, and Jo **burns the brightest.**

Lost in a world of writing and make-believe, Jo is not a *girly girl*, so lady-like innuendos go over her head. At work, Friedrich (her potential love interest) alerts her that her dress is on **fire** while she is tending to one of her brainstorming sessions. At home, while curling Meg's (her lady-like sister) hair, she accidentally **fries** it. She chalks it up to being someone who **"ruins"** everything. While being refined, she *is* hard on delicate things. In a way, she is that **destructive fire, a symbol for Jo's unquenchable spirit. "Her writing is like an attack, moving into enemy territory and occupying space."** Wow! Ultimately, Jo will **not be put out**, even when she tries to be. She will **burn** you even when she doesn't try.

My Least favorite Part - WARNING: SPOILER ALERT There are many tear-jerking moments. (In spite of efforts, death and loss play a major part in the script.) As far as structure, the only question I have is: Is it intentional that Mr. Dashwood (her reluctant and misogynistic publisher) is inserted with dialogue without any transition? He just pops into a scene. This is when the family is realizing that Jo is in love with Friedrich (114). Then, there is also the question: is Jo *being in love* real or "fiction?" There is a bittersweet reveal: It's a story within a story (the story both Jo and Mr. Dashwood "thought was boring") may be playing out. So the reader is left to wonder whether the last set of pages is a figment of Jo's imagination or her actual life? So the end of the script is a bit of you making sense of what is real or fiction.

Effect on the reader: The script: It is an enjoyable anthem for women who need to be empowered. And it is for those who already are empowered but need to be reminded to go boldly after their dream.

These women have the task *or struggle* of self identifying within stringent gender limitations. Throughout the script there is a question I can't help but answer: Whose opinion really counts? These women want to make so many people happy (their parents, their sisters, their town's less fortunate, their future audiences who will enjoy their art, their lovers...AND themselves.) The fact that these little women are fighting to make themselves happy is why the March sisters stand out in a crowd. There are so many critics to please and so many contradictions within a woman. The script highlights the different levels of drive, appreciation, and gratitude—*the full scope of a woman* as they grasp what it means to be one. It also examines the politics within family: Who gets what type of treatment due to *this and that?* These are relatable, real-life problems. -*MW*

Reflect on Multiple POVs of the Same Topic

Bias is like a big bad wolf. It can attack individuals, groups, and even belief systems. Whether you believe they are developed naturally or learned, biases need to be identified and checked to avoid spewing more misconstrued messages, comforting more close-minded patterns, and producing more prejudices in writing.

Similar to the earlier chapter on persuasion, there is an undeniable focus that needs to be placed on diverse thoughts. In the book *They Say, I Say,* Graff and Birkenstein write about "ethical dimension" and the importance of engaging with the ideas of others. The point is "not simply to keep proving and reasserting what they already believe but to stretch what they believe by putting it up against beliefs that differ, sometimes radically, from their own. In an increasingly diverse, global society this is especially crucial to democratic citizenship" (xxviii).

The same school of thought can be applied here. As a thinker and writer, I realize it's always effective to reflect and examine how individual perception or bias in coverage of the same event can influence audiences.

Here, you'll find:
- A **graphic organizer** that will help a student **collect observations** of areas where they were able to distinguish style and detect bias

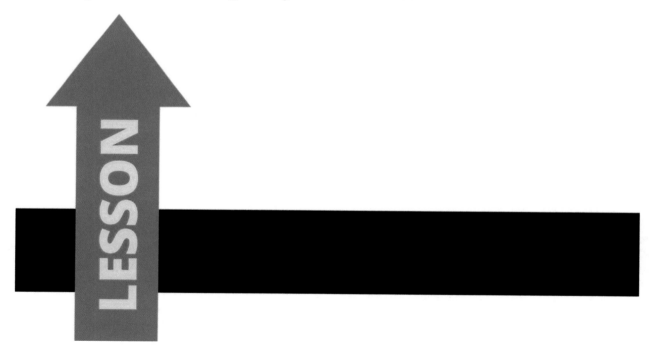

Reflect on Multiple POVs of the Same Topic

Find mainly credible materials/pieces that reflect a wide range of opinions about the topic you are assigned. (Stay away from personal blogs, although I will accept one biased viewpoint.) Gather meaningful details below. Be ready to present your findings.

	Position/ POV because of it	Medium/ Target audience	Tone/Voice/ Style	"Textual Support" (Diction)
Piece 1 TITLE SPEAKER				
Piece 2 TITLE SPEAKER				
Piece 3 TITLE SPEAKER				
Piece 4 TITLE SPEAKER				
Piece 5 TITLE SPEAKER				

Reflect On Your Own Writing

Formulating a plan of action for improvement is important in any classroom. For goal-setting, I rely on business reflective strategies *SWAT and/or SWOT* (strengths, weakness, advantages or opportunities, and threats) in the classroom in order to allow students to reflect on past scores and experiences. This strategic planning technique has been used for individuals and organizations in business, but I think it has its place in the ELA classroom.

In chart form or by making colorful sandwiches, I want students to share their thoughts on a variety of things: strengths, weakness, advantages or opportunities, and threats.

Here, you'll find:
- **Part one -** graphic organizer that allows breakdown of performance
- **Part two -** competition sheet

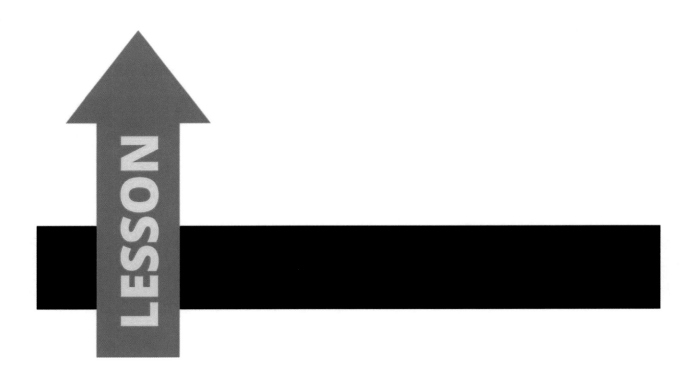

Reflect On Your Writing

List the assignments in your writing folder that you will be rereading and evaluating. Below, record specific details that indicate areas of effectiveness and opportunity.

1.
2.
3.
4.

My Current Strengths	My Current Weaknesses
1.	1.
2.	2.
3.	3.
4.	4.

Create an Action Plan - In complete sentences, identify some of the reasons why your current strengths and weaknesses exist. (What are some of the factors that allow this current state?) Then determine an academic goal for yourself. Express what measurable steps you will take, detailing your strategy for each area that needs improvement and maintenance.

LOOK...

YOU

MADE

IT

HERE

Acknowledgments

Looks like a good place to put a *pen* in it...*no pun intended.*
This picture always gets me. Based on my first years, I can't believe I continued teaching. But I give God all the glory. Teaching is one of the hardest jobs on the planet, and I have always had the utmost respect for those who chose to answer such a calling. I know I could not have made it through my years, let alone a day, without my faith, and some very special people.

I want to take a moment to give thanks. Being a teacher means being a lifelong student. I remember when I used to play school *after school* with elementary friends. The thought of us setting the stuffed animals in chairs, even two old school wooden desks that my grandmother brought home for me, makes me smile. Thank you to those childhood friends, Karen Shields and Deliah Bell (RIP), who sat through me doing my best impressions of my favorite teachers and let me get some practice early on (before I entered the big leagues).

It starts at home for me. I want to thank my grandmother, Marian. May she rest in peace. As a kid, I saw the dedication and commitment she had for the profession and her students even after her retirement. This had a lasting impression on me. Thanks to my mom, Mimi, another teacher, way more popular than I, whose students would stop her while we were out and about to embrace her, update her, introduce her to their family, or even share that they are now teaching *because of her.* Well, Mom, you are an inspiration for me as well. Sitting in your classroom while waiting to walk over to my middle school helped me know, even if I was a little lady, I could teach the big kids. Your warm spirit and love for people is a blessing, and watching you return to the field, even after your retirement, is a testament of your love for teaching.

To the other teachers in my family—too many to name. Love you all (even the ones who are NOT teachers by profession).

I have had some amazing educators. To my favorites - Mrs. Thomas (RIP), Ms. Morris, Mr. Long, Coach Phillips, Mrs. Purnell, Mr. Irving, Ms. Smith, Ms. Tolman, Ms. Colbert, Mrs. Singleton (RIP), Mrs. Traci Mills, Mrs. Debbie Dunlap, Mr. Harambee Taymullah, my first Sunday school teacher, Ms. Rita Washington and my other spiritual teachers and leaders at Metropolitan CME Church and Lakewood Church, THANK YOU for your guidance!

To my editors: I wrote this book during an intense pandemic-stricken time, while teaching AND while in grad school. Though there were days when I felt like I couldn't find enough energy to get through another high-pressure pivot, I knew I had a new support system in my Master of Fine Arts classmates (my MFA fam). I met some awesome people, and one happened to be a fellow scribe/educator, and now sister. Kionna, thank you for being on this journey with me and serving as the editor and consultant. This book was a huge emotional undertaking. Unlike my fiction writing, an escape, this felt more like work. In this testy season, teaching and working from home, I could not have completed this nonfiction project without your expertise, your insight, and your encouragement. Our talks, our prayers were great motivators for me to keep going. Thanks for your patience and your investment during one of the busiest, challenging times in both of our lives. Countdown to graduation!

Geri Felder. *Mama Felder.* What can I say? Thank you for taking time out of your *retirement* to be a trusted reader and editor. I feel special. Your expertise is valued and I am glad we were able to work together on another book! You are amazing!

To all my "teacher" Aunts: Cyndy Covens, Mary Ann Failla, Benita Rogers, Christrina Minor, Evelyn Bonner, Judy Phillips, Joyce Lawson, and Mrs. Mary Durvernay (RIP): thank you for your years of support. Love you.

To my Godmother in education, Mrs. Sandra Cahee, a principal who kept me in the teaching game, may you rest in peace. Words can't express how much I appreciate you seeing me for who I was and accepting me for who I will be. You spoke life into mine when you knew that me being a teacher AND writer go hand-in-hand, and that means so much. You are greatly missed.

I would like to thank educators and leaders in education I have had the pleasure of working side-by-side with, standing on the frontlines, serving kids and those I have met along the way. Shelton Ervin, Milly Mill Delgado, Keisha Smith, Tamika, Tiffany, Kimpson, Mrs. Trotter, Mrs. Biddle, Ms. Mayberry, Gant, Mr. Baker, Wooten, Ron, Mrs. White, Earll Washington, Kiser, Nina, Mr. Blackshire, Laura, Ms. Schawt, Mrs. Allen, Mrs. Heim, Rene, Mrs. Shanks, Nancita Davis, Valerie, Coach B (RIP), Ruqayya, Ingrid Faulk, Marisol, Tyisha, Vicci, Mr. V. Maddox, Mr. T. Fanning, Coach Relvart Smith, Ms. Easter, Mrs. Liptack, Dr. Martinez, Mrs. Flowers, Dr. Ruiz, Mr. Landgrebe, Glen, Sheila Tate, Katrina, Angela H, Robin, Ellen, Kelley Lee, Regina Schaefer, Jennifer S, Ranjani, Angie, Katie, Wells, Demetra, Tanisha, Ms. Baldwin, Page, Jacob Smith, Derrick Atkins, Emily, Barbie, Crystal T, Elaine, Mikki Mims, Krista Glover, Mechelle, Jennifer O, Yolanda Bruce, Crystal A, Leona Aaron, Jacquee Evans, Jacquice Evans, Ms. Wade, Mrs. Cooper, Mrs. Foster, Mrs. Collier, Mrs. Granville, Shante Clark-Davis, Brooke Aseltine, Joel Panda, Lynn Rowland, Mrs. E. Mosley, Mrs. Y. Jackson...and the list goes on...It certainly takes a village...

If it weren't for students, this book could not exist. To those who made teaching enjoyable, who have shared their growth, and allowed me to grow as well, thanks! I am waiting on you to make the world a better place.

To YOU, dear teacher, who have picked up this book and are utilizing it in your class as a travel companion from one component to the next, thank you. I hope this book helps you know you are not alone in this adventure. Though our paths may look different, we are on this journey together.

To my dear cat, Francis. Thank you for always being here at my feet while I write. You are pur-fect!

About the Author

Micole Williams

Micole Williams is a native Houstonian who enjoys being what she calls **lit for life**: *a teacher by profession and a writer by heart!* She is a proud graduate of Prairie View A&M University. For the past 12 years, she has worked as an English Language Arts Teacher. She has taught English I, II, III, IV, English III AP, Yearbook, Professional Communications, Interpersonal Studies, 504/Dyslexia, SAT Prep, and 8th grade Reading STAAR prep. She has also enjoyed creating lessons tailored to her students' needs and being Junior Team Lead. She is currently a virtual learning teacher in her school district.

Outside of teaching, she is the creator and organizer of the BYOBook Club for Busybodies, an author of two fiction books, an indie-filmmaker, and a writer for various online and print magazines and projects.

Areas of expertise include:

For students
- **Strengthening essay writing/increased scores**
- **Creative writing strategies**
- **Close reading mastery**
- **Building a school culture of readers AND writers**

For teachers
- **Student workshops**
- **Teacher workshops**
- **School Program Coordination Consultant**
- **Engaging content creation and curriculum design**
- **Implementing effective classroom management strategies**

To contact Micole about workshops, email her at <u>info@micolewilliams.com</u>.
To order copies, email <u>micole@eclecticallyyou.com</u>.

References

Beers, G. K., & Probst, R. E. (2013). *Notice & note: Strategies for close reading.* Heinemann.

Carroll, J. A., & Wilson, E. E. (2008). *Acts of teaching: How to teach writing: a text, a reader, a narrative* (2nd ed.). Heinemann.

College Entrance Examination Board. (2002). *The AP vertical teams guide for English.*

Crain, H., Swanson, M. C., & Mullen, M. (2013). *The write path: English Language Arts: Exploring Texts with Strategic Reading.* AVID Center.

Daniels, H. (2002). *Literature circles: Voice and choice in book clubs and reading groups.* (2nd ed.). Stenhouse.

Dean, N. (2000). *Voice lessons: Classroom activities to teach diction, detail, imagery, syntax, and tone.* Maupin House.

Degen, M. (2012). *Crafting expository argument: Practical approaches to the writing process for students & teachers.* Telemachos Publishing.

Farah, K. (2020, March 20). *4 Tips for Teachers Shifting to Teaching Online.* Edutopia. https://www.edutopia.org/article/4-tips-supporting-learning-home.

Gallagher, K., & Kittle, P. (2018). *180 Days: Two teachers and the quest to engage and empower adolescents.* Heinemann.

Graff, G., Birkenstein, C., & Durst, R. K. (2015). *"They say / I say": The moves that matter in academic writing, with readings.* W.W. Norton & Company.

Harwayne, S., Calkins, L., & Little, J. (1991). *Living between the lines.* Heinemann Educational Books, Inc.

Heinrichs, J. (2013). *Thank you for arguing: What Aristotle, Lincoln, and Homer Simpson can teach us about the art of persuasion.* Three Rivers Press.

Lunsford, A. A., & Ruskiewicz, J. J. (2019). *Everything's an argument.* Bedford/St Martin's.

Marzano, R. J. (2004). *Building background knowledge for academic achievement: Research on what works in schools.* Association for Supervision and Curriculum Development.

Glossary of literary terms

Alliteration the repetition of the same initial consonants of words or of stressed syllables in any sequence of neighboring words

Allusion an indirect or passing reference to an event, person, place, or artistic work

Anaphora a rhetorical device that consists of repeating a sequence of words at the beginnings of neighboring clauses, thereby lending them emphasis

Analogy comparing two things or instances in time often based on their structure and used to explain a complex idea in simpler terms

Conflict the problem or opposing force created; basic types: Man vs. self, man, nature, society, and technology

Connotation refers to the wide array of personal or emotional associations that help define the word

Consonance repetition of consonant sounds two or more times in short succession within a sentence or phrase

Denotation is the precise, literal definition of a word that might be found in a dictionary

Diction refers to the author's word choice

Ellipsis when one or more words are omitted from a sentence

Ethos a characteristic spirit of a given culture, era, or community or its beliefs; Ethos, in purely rhetorical terms, is a label used to identify an appeal to the ethics of a culture or individual

Expository writing a neutral-positioned composition aiming to inform or explain

Foreshadowing literary device in which a writer gives an advance hint or clue of what is to come later in the story

Hyperbole an intentionally exaggerated statement or claim not meant to be taken literally but creating a desired humorous effect

Idiom a phrase or expression that typically presents a figurative, non-literal meaning attached to the phrase

Imagery visually descriptive or figurative language **sensory imagery** appeals to the senses—touch, sight, smell, etc

Irony the expression of one's meaning by using language that normally signifies the opposite of what the writer intends to achieve a humorous effect or to add emphasis

Jargon a specialized terminology associated with a particular field or area of activity

Juxtaposition the intentional act of placing two elements side by side in order to contrast the two

Motif any recurring element that has symbolic significance in a story

Onomatopoeia the formation of a word from a sound associated with what is named

Oxymoron a figure of speech in which apparently contradictory terms appear in conjunction, a juxtaposed construction

Pathos a quality that appeals to high (evokes happiness and comfort) and/or low emotions (evokes pity or sadness)

Paradox a seemingly absurd or self-contradictory statement or proposition that when investigated or explained may prove to be well-founded or true

Persuasive essay a one-sided argument that aims to influence

Personification the attribution of a personal nature or human characteristic to a nonhuman or the representation of an abstract quality in human form

Pun a play on words that exploits multiple meanings of a term, or of similar-sounding words, for an intended humorous or rhetorical effect

Rhetorical Question a question not asked in order to receive an answer but posed to make a point

Symbol/Symbolism A thing or concrete item that represents or stands for an abstract idea

Syntax sentence structure

Theme the central message, moral of the story

Thesis statement the controlling idea

Tone the author's attitude toward the subject

Voice the distinct, individual style in which a certain author writes his or her works

ABOUT THE BOOK

In *Miss Lit for Life Lessons for High School English Teachers by a High School English Teacher*, you will find engaging and effective modern-day ELA lessons to add to your tool kit! Inspired by student needs and the world around us, the crafted challenges for 21st Century learners can be applied outside the classroom and in the real world. This book was shaped by verbal and written student-input about what worked best and helped them increase in skills and scores. Micole Williams has defined, planned, and designed a journey for fellow teachers and their diverse learners across grade levels.

Candidly, she shares two types of lessons:

> 1. Those learned while teaching and

> 2. Those she designed and developed for her diverse students each year.

Here, in 5 chapters, you will find a string of her most impactful, tried-and-true challenges that you can use *as is* or adapt to your path along the course of a year.

- The adventure begins at Crossing Genres where you will find resources to set you off in the right direction.
- Things get deep on Highway Analysis. Sharpen insight with tools that are practical to use.
- It's time to get lit at Story Central. Delve into ways to engage readers, ignite writers, and let the imagination run wild.
- On Persuasive Parkway explore matters of the heart that allow for students to perfect their argumentative skills, so they can effectively fight for what they are passionate about.
- At Reflection Avenue, you'll find a special time to look back on the journey in order to effectively move forward to the next.

Miss Lit for Life Lessons provides writing prompts, manageable exercises, discussion questions, and graphic organizers that can be successfully implemented in any curriculum.

Made in the USA
Middletown, DE
07 November 2020